Easy
Chinese
Cookbook

Simple & Delicious Chinese Food Recipes for Beginners and Advanced Users

Traci Lockhart

Table of Contents

Introduction

Chinese cuisine is an important part of Chinese culture, which includes cuisines from different parts of China as well as overseas Chinese who have settled in other parts of the world. Due to the Chinese diaspora and the country's historic power, Chinese cuisine has influenced many other Asian cuisines, with modifications made to suit local palates. Chinese staples such as rice, dumplings, noodles, barley, Chinese wonton, and tofu as well as utensils such as chopsticks and woks can now be found all over the world.

Preferences for seasoning and cooking techniques in Chinese provinces depend on differences in historical context and ethnic groups. Geographical features such as mountains, rivers, forests and deserts also have a strong influence on the local ingredients available, as China's climate varies from tropical in the south to subarctic in the northeast. Imperial and aristocratic preferences also play a role in the evolution of Chinese cuisine. Due to imperial expansion and trade, ingredients and cooking techniques from other cultures have been incorporated into Chinese cuisines over time.

The most praised Four Great Traditions are Chuan, Lu, Yue, and Huaiyang, representing cuisines of West, North, South, and East China, respectively. The modern Eight Cuisines of China are Anhui (徽菜; Huīcài), Guangdong (粤菜; Yuècài), Fujian (闽菜; Mǐncài), Hunan (湘菜; Xiāngcài), Jiangsu (苏菜; Sūcài), Shandong (鲁菜; Lǔcài), Sichuan (川菜; Chuāncài), and Zhejiang (浙菜; Zhècài) cuisines.

Color, smell and taste are the three traditional aspects used to describe Chinese food as well as the meaning, appearance and nutritional value of the food. The degree of doneness must be appreciated according to the ingredients used, the work with the knife, the cooking time and the seasoning.

The 8 Culinary Traditions of China

Chinese cuisine is as diverse as its culture, with each region writing a new menu. Cooking styles, ingredients, flavors - they all differ from region to region. The best-known regional cuisines in China are Anhui, Cantonese, Fujian, Hunan, Jiangsu, Shandong, Sichuan, and Zhejiang.

Cantonese cuisine is known around the world for its distinctive style. Most of the dishes are steamed and fried, which makes them healthy and non-greasy. The dishes here are tender, slightly sweet and have a sweet scent. **Shandong cuisine** has its origins in eastern China and is characterized mainly by seafood, as it is a coastal province. You can find scallops, shrimp, clams, sea cucumbers and just about anything on the menu. They depend heavily on salty flavors.

Zhejiang cuisine also feeds on seafood, but focuses more on sweet and fresh flavors. Their food is known to have a tender appearance. They also like to use bamboo shoots. This province is famous for being the "land of milk and honey". Likewise, the dishes of the Jiangsu region are known for their creamy texture. In the past, it was an important part of the royal cuisine of ancient China. Their dishes offer a balanced mix of sweet and savory flavors.

Szechuan cuisine is characterized by its strong, lively and spicy aromas. The use of Sichuan peppercorns makes it unique. It's for those of you who love the sting.

Anhui cuisine uses a wide variety of herbs and vegetables, especially fresh bamboo and mushrooms. It also uses many wild herbs to enhance the taste and aroma.

Fujian cuisine is often served in broth or soup with cooking styles such as braising, stewing, stewing and boiling. The most notable characteristics of this cuisine are: the use of fresh ingredients from the mountains and the sea, the preparation of soups and great attention to spices.

Hunan cuisine is known for its spicy taste, fresh aroma and deep color. This province is known as the "Land of Fish and Rice". It is famous for its stews, but its cuisine also offers many grilled and baked dishes.

History and Developments of Chinese Cuisine

China is one of the oldest civilizations on the planet and has been a leader on the Asian continent for the past 4 millennia, not only in terms of developing new technologies, but also expanding its influence, not only religion, fashion and customs, but also culinary.

As one of the first Asian civilizations to achieve stability and steady growth, China quickly managed to develop a very specific taste in food which allowed its cuisine to develop and change at an incredible rate. This great attention to food today can be attributed to several factors that enabled Chinese chefs to create the most diverse and interesting cuisine in the world: the rapid spread of Han culture from the Yellow River across China, which spans many climates, as their own indigenous ingredients and culinary traditions, the constant absorption of foreign culinary traditions through relationships or commercial expansions, a very popular movement that herbal medicine has instilled in the kitchen , which made the preparation of food very balanced and healthy, and finally endless changes in culinary fashions imposed by the Chinese imperial courts and elites.

Preparation of Chinese Food

Chinese cuisine is famous all over the world. Not only does it have a reputation for being delicious, it is also considered an art form in its own right. Chinese cuisine is about examining the combination of ingredients and paying special attention to the complex process and associated equipment. Different ingredients are cooked using different methods, while the same ingredient can be used in different dishes to create different flavors and appearances. There are hundreds of cooking methods in China. However, the most common methods are stirring, frying, light frying, braising, boiling, steaming, and broiling.

Stir-frying

The most commonly used method is stir-frying. With this method, the processed ingredients are cooked over high heat for a short time. Food oil is used as a heat conductor. Usually a wok is used over high heat, cooking oil is added, followed by the ingredients and seasoning. Due to the short processing time, the ingredients largely retain their nutritional value. Fried meat is generally juicy and flavourful, and the vegetables are generally tender and crisp.

Deep-frying

Much more cooking oil is used in deep frying than in light frying (the ingredient must be completely submerged in the oil), resulting in foods with a crisp texture. The common way to prepare dishes for frying is to cut the ingredients into chunks or medium sized pieces, soak them for a while in the prepared seasonings, cover them with cornstarch (optional) and finally toss them. Fry in hot oil over medium heat. The density of the coating determines the freshness and tenderness of the ingredients used inside and out.

Roasting

During cooking, food is cooked over a charcoal flame or in an oven. Moisture is removed from food, spices are effaced from the outside. The outside of grilled food becomes drier and browner, but the flavors are retained and intensified. There are many ingredients that can be grilled, including all types of meat, as well as most root vegetables and onions. When grilling food, the ingredients should be cleaned, seasoned and drizzled with cooking oil to reduce the loss of moisture from the ingredients during the cooking process.

Steaming

A special cooking method invented in China is steam. It is widely used for steaming buns and dumplings in northern China, where people rely on wheat-based food. In this process, the ingredients are placed in a steamer basket which is placed over the water in a steamer pot. Steamed foods contain more nutrients than cooked foods because less nutrients are filtered out in the water. Very little cooking oil and spices are used (most Chinese only cook steamed beaten eggs with salt), so that the natural taste of food is preserved and even improved.

Braising

To cook large ingredients that melt in your mouth, braise means adding the ingredients and spices to a wok or saucepan at the same time, adding water, bringing to a boil, then simmering for an hour or more. The ingredients are usually cut into cubes or diamonds. For cooking stews, the ingredients, especially those of animal origin, should be freed from the fishy smell in boiling water and first rinsed with clean water, and the sauce should be thickened with cornstarch or finally brought to a boil.

Crunchy Scallion Pancakes

Prep Time: 20 minutes.
Cook Time: 10 minutes.
Serves: 2
Ingredients:
For the dough
- 1 cup all-purpose flour, about + extra for dusting
- ½ cup boiling water,

For the filling
- 1 tablespoon coconut oil or melted lard
- 1 tablespoon plain flour
- ⅛ teaspoon ground Sichuan pepper, or Chinese five-spice powder
- ⅛ teaspoon salt, or to taste
- 2 stalks scallions

For frying
- 2 tablespoons cooking oil

Preparation:
1. Put the flour in a heatproof bowl. Pour in boiling water. Stir with a pair of toothpicks or a fork until the flour turns into small pieces and no more water is visible.
2. Once cool enough to handle, knead the mixture into a smooth dough. Let stand 30 minutes.
3. Prepare the garnish: mix flour, ground Sichuan pepper (or five spice powder), salt with coconut oil (or melted lard). Finely chop the chives.

Shape pancakes:
4. Knead the dough again. Then press it flat with a rolling pin into a thin rectangle (sprinkle with flour to prevent it from sticking).
5. Spread the coconut mixture evenly over the dough. Sprinkle with scallions.
6. Roll the dough into a string (on the shorter side). Cut into 4 cylinders.
7. Put a piece at one end. Roll to desired thickness.

Fry the pancakes:
8. Heat the oil in a pan over high heat. Place the pancakes, then reduce the heat to medium.
9. Turn 2-3 times. Cook until both sides are golden brown.

Serving Suggestion: Serve the scallion pancakes with dipping sauce.
Variation Tip: Use lard in case not having coconut oil.

Nutritional Information Per Serving:
Calories 355| Fat 14.2g |Sodium 5mg | Carbs 49.3g | Fiber 2.6g | Sugar 0.6g | Protein 7g

Flavorful Egg Pancakes

Prep Time: 15 minutes
Cook Time: 9 minutes
Servings: 12
Ingredients:
- 1¾ cups unbleached all-purpose flour, plus more for dusting
- ¾ cup boiling water
- ½ cup cold water
- 1 tablespoon sesame oil, toasted

Preparation:
1. In a bowl, place the flour.
2. Slowly add the boiling water, stirring continuously until a shaggy dough ball form.
3. Place the dough ball onto a lightly floured surface and with your hands until smooth ball forms.
4. With a damp kitchen towel, cover the dough ball and set aside at room temperature for at least 30 minutes.
5. Uncover the dough ball and again knead until smooth.
6. Place the dough ball onto a lightly floured surface and then roll into a 12-inch-long log.
7. With a sharp knife, cut the dough roll into 12 equal-sized pieces.
8. With lightly floured hands, flatten each dough piece into 2-inch rounds.
9. Spread oil on 1 side of each dough round.
10. Make a pair of dough rounds by pressing lightly oiled sides together.
11. With a floured rolling pin, roll each dough pair into a 7-inch pancake, flipping over now and again to roll evenly on both sides.
12. Heat an ungreased cast-iron skillet over medium-high heat and cook 1 pancake for about 1 minute or until light golden.
13. Carefully flip the pancake and cook for about 30 seconds or until light golden.
14. Transfer the pancakes onto a plate.
15. Carefully separate the pancake into 2 thin pancakes.
16. Repeat with remaining pancakes.
17. Serve warm.

Serving Suggestions: Serve alongside the lettuce.
Variation Tip: Use the wooden spoon to mix the flour with water.

Nutritional Information per Serving:
Calories: 76 | Fat: 1.3g|Sat Fat: 0.2g|Carbohydrates: 13.9g|Fiber: 0.5g|Sugar: 0.1g|Protein: 1.9g

Youtiao (Doughnut Sticks)

Prep Time: 20 minutes.
Cook Time: 15 minutes.
Serves: 5
Ingredients:
- 200g all-purpose flour
- 1 teaspoon baking powder
- ⅛ teaspoon baking soda, optional
- ¼ teaspoon salt
- 1 egg, lightly beaten, plus water combined
- 1 tablespoon neutral cooking oil, plus some for coating

Preparation:
Make the dough
1. With a food processor: add the flour, baking powder, baking soda (if using), salt, the mixture of eggs, water and oil to the bowl. Mix and knead on low speed for about 8 minutes. Rub a little oil in your hands (so that it does not stick) and remove the paste.
2. Manual - Use a silicone spatula to mix and match all the ingredients into a coarse-looking paste. Cover and let stand 15 minutes. Cover your hands with oil (to prevent sticking). Squeeze the dough with your fist. Then fold the dough sideways towards the middle with your fingers. Repeat the movement until the dough is smooth (it should be soft but not sticky at this point).
Let the dough rest
3. Divide the dough into two equal portions. Shape each into a smooth ball. Cover with oil then cover with cling film.
4. Let the dough rest for 2 to 4 hours at room temperature. Or store in the refrigerator overnight. Wait at least 1 hour the next morning until it has come back to room temperature.
Shapes of sticks
5. Before handling the dough, start heating the frying oil.
6. Transfer the pieces of dough to your floured work surface (or cutting board). Use your hands to flatten each piece into a rectangle (approximately 4 × 10 inches / 10 × 25 cm). Remember not to knead it again, but to handle it with care.
7. Lightly dust the dough with flour to prevent it from sticking. Then cut each piece into 10 equal strips.
8. Put one strip on the other. Use a toothpick to press the center lengthwise to join them. Repeat the operation with the remaining dough pieces (sprinkle with flour if necessary).
Fry the chopsticks
9. Once the oil reaches 190 ° C / 374 ° F, lower the heat to minimum. Spread the dough delicately then immerse it delicately in the oil (be careful not to splash).
10. As it rises to the surface, rotate it continuously with a pair of toothpicks. As soon as the dough has stopped swelling and is evenly browned, place it on a plate lined with paper towels (to soak up the excess oil).
11. Repeat to cook the rest of the dough. You can cook two sticks at the same time, but you can no longer fry them at the same time, as this will reduce the temperature of the oil too much.
Serving Suggestion: Serve the Toutiao with ketchup.
Variation Tip: Use almond flour as substitute of all-purpose flour.
Nutritional Information Per Serving:
Calories 184 | Fat 3.7g |Sodium 88mg | Carbs 29.9g | Fiber 1.4g | Sugar 1.2g | Protein 6.9g

Tender Steamed Eggs with Chives

Prep Time: 05 minutes.
Cook Time: 10 minutes.
Serves: 4
Ingredients:
- 4 eggs, beaten
- Warm water, double volume of the beaten eggs (see step 1 & 2)
- 1 pinch salt
- 2 teaspoons chive, finely chopped (optional)
- 4 teaspoons light soy sauce
- 4 drop sesame oil

Preparation:
1. Pour lukewarm water over the beaten eggs. Add salt and mix well.
2. Pour the mixture through a sieve into 2 small serving bowls. Sprinkle with chives when using.
3. Cover the bowls with cling film. Pierce with a toothpick to allow steam to escape.
4. Steam over low heat for 10-12 minutes (place the bowls when the water starts to boil).
5. Season with light soy sauce and sesame oil (if desired, chop the cottage cheese several times so that the sauce can penetrate). Serve hot.
6. If you are using an extra garnish: Steam the egg as usual for 7 minutes, then place it on the shrimp and vegetables. Steam for another 3 minutes.
Serving Suggestion: Serve with chopped green onions on the top.
Variation Tip: Use milk instead of water to make milk steamed egg as you desired.
Nutritional Information Per Serving:
Calories 249 | Fat 16.2g |Sodium 632mg | Carbs 13.9g | Fiber 1.9g | Sugar 2.2g | Protein 16.9g

Chicken Congee with Mushrooms

Prep Time: 05 minutes.
Cook Time: 15 minutes.
Serves: 4
Ingredients:
• 200g raw rice, medium or short grain, about 1 cup
• 1200ml boiling water, about 5 cups
• 4 dried shiitake mushrooms, rehydrated & thinly sliced
• ½ teaspoon salt
• 1-inch ginger, minced
• 2 teaspoons chives, finely chopped (optional)
For the chicken
• 1-piece chicken breast, cut into narrow strips/thin slices, about 5.3oz
• 1 teaspoon light soy sauce
• 1 teaspoon oyster sauce
• ½ teaspoon Shaoxing rice wine
• ½ teaspoon corn-starch
• ½ teaspoon sesame oil
• 1 pinch ground white pepper
• 1 pinch salt
• 1 pinch sugar
Preparation:
Freeze rice
1. The day before the congee is cooked, rinse the rice under running water. Drain then transfer to a plastic container / bag. Freeze overnight.
2. Soak the dried shiitake mushrooms in water overnight.
Boil rice
3. Pour boiling water into a saucepan. Put the frozen rice. Add salt, mushrooms, and the water the mushrooms have been soaked in (it's full of umami flavor).
4. As soon as it starts to boil again, lower the heat to minimum.
5. Cover with a lid and simmer for 10 minutes.
Marinate the chicken
6. While waiting for the rice to cook. Marinate the chicken with all the ingredients listed.
Chicken cooking
7. Add the chicken strips and ginger. Cook for 1 minute then turn off the heat.
8. Let stand (covered) for another 1 minute.
Assemble the plate
9. Add the chives to the congee. Mix well then transfer to serving bowls.

10. Optional garnish: Cover each bowl with half a hard-boiled egg and a few toasted peanuts. Serve hot.
Serving Suggestion: Serve the congee with crushed, toasted peanuts.
Variation Tip: Replace the chicken with smoked tofu.
Nutritional Information Per Serving:
Calories 149 | Fat 1.2g |Sodium 1632mg | Carbs 23.9g | Fiber 1.7g | Sugar 5.2g | Protein 8.6g

Stir-fried Eggs & Tomato

Prep Time: 10 minutes
Cook Time: 7 minutes
Servings: 4
Ingredients:
• 1 pound tomatoes, cut into small wedges
• 1 scallion, chopped finely
• 4 eggs
• 1 teaspoon Shaoxing wine
• ½ teaspoon sesame oil
• Salt, taste
• ¼ ground white pepper
• 3 tablespoons vegetable oil, divided
• 2 teaspoons sugar
• ¼-½ cup water
Preparation:
1. In a bowl, add eggs, wine, sesame oil, salt and white pepper and beat until well combined.
2. In a skillet, heat 2 tablespoons of oil over medium heat.
3. Add the egg mixture and cook for about 2 minutes, stirring continuously.
4. Transfer the scrambled eggs onto a plate and set aside.
5. In the same skillet, heat the remaining oil over high heat and stir fry the tomatoes and scallions for about 1 minute.
6. Add sugar, salt and water and stir to combine.
7. Stir in the cooked eggs and cook, covered for about 1-2 minutes or until the tomatoes are softened completely.
8. Uncover the skillet and stir fry for about 1-2 minutes or until the sauce thickens.
9. Serve hot.
Serving Suggestions: Toasted bread will go great with this stir fry.
Variation Tip: Use ripe but firm tomatoes.
Nutritional Information per Serving:
Calories: 189 | Fat: 15.4g|Sat Fat: 3.5g|Carbohydrates: 7.6g|Fiber: 1.5g|Sugar: 5.7g|Protein: 6.6g

Marinated Tea Eggs

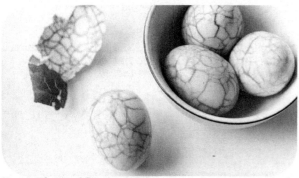

Prep Time: 05 minutes.
Cook Time: 20 minutes.
Serves: 8
Ingredients:
- 8 eggs, at room temperature
- 2 bag black tea
- 1 teaspoon Chinese five-spice powder
- 4 teaspoons soy sauce
- ½ tablespoon rock sugar, or granulated sugar
- 2 teaspoons salt

Preparation:
1. Place the eggs in a pot of cold water (enough to cover them). Bring the water to a boil, then lower the heat. Simmer for 6 minutes.
2. Drain the eggs then cool them under running water. When cool enough to touch, use the back of a spoon to gently crack the eggshells.
3. Return the eggs to a clean saucepan. Add all other ingredients and enough water to cover the eggs. Bring the water to a boil, then lower the heat. Cook over low heat for 10 minutes.
4. Transfer everything to a container. Let stand for at least 12 hours. You can store the eggs in the refrigerator for up to 4 days.
5. If you prefer to eat hot eggs, simply heat the egg in the liquid.
Serving Suggestion: Serve the Marinated tea eggs with peanuts.
Variation Tip: Use individual spices of your choice if not getting Chinese five-spice powder.
Nutritional Information Per Serving:
Calories 68 | Fat 4.4g | Sodium 795mg | Carbs 1.5g | Fiber 0g | Sugar 1.1g | Protein 5.7g

Chicken Rice Congee

Prep Time: 15 minutes
Cook Time: 1 hour 5 minutes
Servings: 6
Ingredients:
- 8 cups water
- 1 cup long-grain white rice, rinsed and drained
- 6 bone-in chicken thighs
- 1 (1-inch) piece fresh ginger, sliced into large pieces
- Salt, to taste

Preparation:
1. In a large Dutch oven, add water, rice, chicken thighs and ginger over high heat and bring to a boil.
2. Reduce the heat to medium-low and cook, covered for about 1 hour, stirring occasionally.
3. With a slotted spoon, transfer the chicken thighs into a bowl.
4. With 2 forks, shred the meat and discard the bones.
5. Add the shredded meat and salt into the rice mixture and stir to combine.
6. Serve hot.
Serving Suggestions: Serve with the topping of boiled eggs, ginger slices and scallion.
Variation Tip: The addition of goji berries will enhance the taste of congee.
Nutritional Information per Serving:
Calories: 329 | Fat: 8.6g | Sat Fat: 2.4g | Carbohydrates: 24.9g | Fiber: 0.4g | Sugar: 0.1g | Protein: 35g

Baozi (Steamed Buns)

Prep Time: 10 minutes.
Cook Time: 15 minutes.
Serves: 6
Ingredients:
- 250g all-purpose/plain flour
- 1 teaspoon dried active yeast
- ¾ teaspoon baking powder
- 1 tablespoon sugar, or to taste
- 130ml lukewarm water
- 4 Chinese dates, for flower-shaped buns, optional

Preparation:
1. FOR THE HANDS: Combine the flour, baking powder, baking powder and sugar. Gradually add water. Mix with toothpicks / spatula until no loose flour is visible. Put them together and knead briefly into a dough. Let stand (covered) for 10 minutes. Knead again very gently.
2. WHEN KNITTING WITH A STAND MIXER: Combine the flour, baking powder, baking powder, sugar and water in the bowl. Knead at low speed until obtaining a very smooth dough (about 8 minutes).
Shape rolls
3. IF YOU ARE MAKING SMALL ROUNDS: Divide the dough into 6 parts (4 pieces if you prefer larger buns). Knead the piece of dough and fold it towards the center of the ball, so as to create a smooth outer surface. Roll the ball between your hands to form a slightly raised shape.
4. IF YOU ARE MAKING SMALL FLOWERS: Divide the dough into 4 parts. Wrap a piece in a long, thin string. Fold the two ends into a "J" shape in opposite

directions. Twist each end towards the middle of the rope until they meet.

5. Take a pair of toothpicks, place one on each side (in the middle) and pinch them together to form a flower. Place a Chinese date in the center of the flower.

6. Let the rolls rest.

7. Place the rolls in the steamer basket (line them up with steamer paper or apply a thin layer of oil to prevent sticking). Make sure there is enough space between each loaf.

8. Let stand for about 30 minutes. Rested rollers should be slightly larger (not twice as large) and very smooth on the surface. If you press lightly, the dough will crack.

Steam the rolls

9. Place the steamer basket in a saucepan / wok filled with cold water. Start cooking over high heat.

10. Low to medium-low after the water is completely boiled. Allow 10 minutes from this point (add 2 minutes if your buns are larger). Serve hot.

Serving Suggestion: Serve the Chinese steamed buns with soup.

Variation Tip: Use almond flour if you want low carb.

Nutritional Information Per Serving:
Calories 162 | Fat 0.4g |Sodium 2mg | Carbs 34.9g | Fiber 1.3g | Sugar 2.1g | Protein 4.6g

Tasty Scallion Crepes

Prep Time: 15 minutes
Cook Time: 14 minutes
Servings: 9
Ingredients:
• ¾ cup all-purpose flour
• ¼ teaspoon salt
• ⅛ teaspoon ground white pepper
• 1 cup water
• 3 medium eggs
• 2 scallions, chopped finely
• 2 tablespoons vegetable oil
Preparation:
1. In a mixing bowl, add flour, salt, and white pepper and mix well.
2. Add water and mix until well combined.
3. Add eggs and scallions and mix until smooth.
4. Heat a non-stick skillet over medium heat.
5. Add about 4 tablespoons of the mixture and with a spatula, spread in an even layer.
6. Cook for about 30-40 seconds or until golden brown.

7. Carefully flip the crepe and cook for about 30-40 seconds or until golden brown.
8. Repeat with the remaining mixture.
9. Serve warm.
Serving Suggestions: Serve these crepes with Chinese chili oil, black bean sauce or sweet soy sauce.
Variation Tip: You can mix the batter the night before and store in the refrigerator. Stir very well before using.
Nutritional Information per Serving:
Calories: 87 | Fat: 4.6g|Sat Fat: 1.1g|Carbohydrates: 8.3g|Fiber: 0.4g|Sugar: 0.2g|Protein: 3g

Steamed Shrimp and Egg

Prep Time: 15 minutes
Cook Time: 37 minutes
Servings: 4
Ingredients:
• 4 eggs
• 1 cup cooked small shrimp
• 8 ounces fresh bean sprouts
• ⅓ cup scallions, sliced thinly
• ¼ teaspoon garlic powder
• 2 tablespoons vegetable oil
• 3 cups chicken broth
• 2 tablespoons soy sauce
• 2 tablespoons distilled white vinegar
• 2 tablespoons sugar
• 2 tablespoons corn-starch
Preparation:
1. In a bowl, add the eggs, shrimp, bean sprouts, scallions and garlic powder and mix until well combined.
2. In a skillet, heat the oil over medium heat.
3. Place about ½ cup of the egg mixture into the skillet and shape into a patty.
4. Cook for about 4 minutes per side or until golden brown.
5. Transfer the patty onto a plate.
6. Repeat with the remaining egg mixture.
7. In a saucepan, add the remaining ingredients and beat until well combined.
8. Place the pan over medium-low heat and cook for about 5 minutes or until the sauce thickens, stirring frequently.
9. Place the sauce over patties and serve.
Serving Suggestions: Serve alongside fresh greens.
Variation Tip: Make sure to use small-sized shrimp.
Nutritional Information per Serving:
Calories: 282 | Fat: 13.5g|Sat Fat: 3.3g|Carbohydrates: 15.3g|Fiber: 0.3g|Sugar: 7.3g|Protein: 25.2g

Pork Meatballs Congee

Prep Time: 20 minutes
Cook Time: 50 minutes
Servings: 6
Ingredients:
- ½ pound ground pork
- 2 tablespoons fish sauce
- 1 tablespoon soy sauce
- Freshly ground white pepper, to taste
- 8 cups chicken broth
- 1 cup jasmine rice
- 1 lemongrass stalk, cut into 3-inch pieces and crushed
- 5 dried red chiles, stemmed
- ¼ cup vegetable oil
- 5 garlic cloves, sliced thinly
- ¼ cup distilled white vinegar
- 1 Serrano chile, seeded and minced
- ½ teaspoon sugar

Preparation:
1. In a bowl, add the pork, fish sauce, soy sauce and a pinch of white pepper and mix until well combined.
2. Set aside for about 15-30 minutes.
3. In a cast-iron pan, add the broth, rice and lemongrass pieces over medium-high heat and bring to a boil.
4. Reduce the heat to low and simmer partially, covered for about 25 minutes.
5. Meanwhile, heat a small skillet over medium heat and toast the dried chiles for about 3 minutes, stirring continuously.
6. Transfer the dried chiles to a spice grinder and grind until roughly powdered.
7. With paper towels, wipe out the skillet.
8. In the same skillet, heat the oil over low heat and cook the garlic for about 10 minutes or until caramelized, stirring frequently.
9. Transfer the garlic oil into a small bowl and set aside.
10. In another small bowl, add the vinegar, Serrano and sugar and stir until the sugar is dissolved.
11. With a small ice cream scooper, make about 1-inch meatballs with the pork mixture.
12. Discard the lemongrass from rice mixture and drop in the meatballs.
13. Increase the heat to medium-high and simmer covered heat for about 10 minutes, stirring occasionally.
14. Serve hot.
Serving Suggestions: Serve with the topping of fried eggs, scallion and chili oil.
Variation Tip: The uncooked meatballs can be refrigerated overnight.
Nutritional Information per Serving:
Calories: 303 | Fat: 12.2g|Sat Fat: 2.7g|Carbohydrates: 27g|Fiber: 1.5g|Sugar: 1.6g|Protein: 19g

Scallion Omelet with Bean Sprouts

Prep Time: 10 minutes
Cook Time: 6 minutes
Servings: 4
Ingredients:
- 6 large eggs, beaten
- ½ teaspoon Maggi seasoning
- Salt and ground white pepper, to taste
- ½ cup bean sprouts
- ¼ cup carrot, peeled and grated
- 3 scallions, sliced
- 1 tablespoon vegetable oil

Preparation:
1. In a bowl, add the eggs, Maggi seasoning, salt and white pepper and beat until well combined.
2. Add bean sprouts, carrots and scallions and stir to combine.
3. In a large skillet, heat the oil over medium heat.
4. Add the egg mixture and with the spatula, spread evenly.
5. Cook for about 3 minutes, tilting the pan occasionally to let the uncooked mixture flow underneath.
6. Carefully flip the omelet and cook for about 2-3 minutes or until omelet is done completely.
Serving Suggestions: Serve with your favorite dipping sauce.
Variation Tip: You can replace scallion with Chinese chives too.
Nutritional Information per Serving:
Calories: 152 | Fat: 11g|Sat Fat: 3g|Carbohydrates: 3.3g|Fiber: 0.5g|Sugar: 1.2g|**Protein:** 10.7g

Stir-Fried Noodles with Marinated Chicken

Prep Time: 15 minutes.
Cook Time: 10 minutes.
Serves: 4
Ingredients:
• 8 ounces chicken breast
For the Marinade:
• 2 teaspoons dark soy sauce
• 2 teaspoons Chinese rice wine or dry sherry
• ½ teaspoon salt
• Black pepper (or white pepper, freshly ground to taste)
• 1 pinch corn-starch
For the Stir-Fry:
• ½ pound Shanghai-style noodles
• 1 ½ teaspoons sesame oil (or as needed)
• 1 cup cabbage (shredded)
• 1 large clove garlic (peeled and minced)
• 1 spring onion (cut into 1-inch pieces)
• 6 tablespoons oil (divided, for stir-frying, or as needed)
• 1 tablespoon hoisin sauce (mixed with 1 ½ tablespoons water)
• Optional: additional soy sauce, salt, or sugar (for seasonings, as desired)
Preparation:
1. Cut the chicken into 1-inch or bite-sized cubes (or you can cut the chicken into slices or strips).
2. In a large bowl, combine the dark soy sauce, rice wine, salt, pepper and corn-starch. Add the chicken pieces, turn them well and let marinate for 20 minutes.
3. While the chicken marinates, prepare the rest of the ingredients.
4. In a large pot, cook the noodles in boiling water, stirring, until the noodles is soft but still firm (al dente). Drain well. Rinse with cold water, drain again, drizzle with sesame oil and set aside.
5. Wash and finely chop the cabbage and store it.
6. Peel and chop the garlic. Cut the chives into 1-inch pieces and set aside; the onion is used at the end of the preparation.
7. In a wok or skillet, heat 2 ½ tablespoons of oil over medium-high heat. When the oil is hot, add the garlic. Fry until fragrant (about 30 seconds). Add the chicken pieces. Fry until they turn white and are almost done. Take out of the wok.
8. Heat 2 tablespoons of oil in a wok. When the oil is hot, add the cabbage. Fry for 2 minutes. If desired, season with a little soy sauce and / or sugar when frying. Take out of the wok.

9. Heat 1 ½ tablespoon of oil in a wok. When the oil is hot, add the noodles. Stir quickly to coat the noodles with oil and make sure it doesn't stick to the pan.
10. Add the hoisin sauce and stir again to coat the noodles. Season to taste and season with salt and / or soy sauce. Add the cooked chicken and cabbage and mix well.
11. Pour the hoisin sauce into the wok and add the chicken and cabbage.
12. Add the scallion and mix well to make sure all the ingredients are hot.
13. Serve hot and enjoy!
Serving Suggestion: Serve the egg & scallion crepe with chili garlic sauce.
Variation Tip: Use grated courgette/zucchini, grated carrot or coarsely chopped spinach (briefly blanched) are great choices.
Nutritional Information Per Serving:
Calories 66 | Fat 2.8g |Sodium 78mg | Carbs 7.5g | Fiber 0.3g | Sugar 0.2g | Protein 2.7g

Stir-Fried Noodles

Prep Time: 05 minutes.
Cook Time: 15 minutes.
Serves: 4
Ingredients:
• 16 ounces' noodles (Hong Kong, or 10 to 12 ounces fine dried egg noodles)
• 1 tablespoon coconut oil
• 3 tablespoons peanut oil (or vegetable oil; or as needed)
Preparation:
1. Put enough water in a large pot to cover the noodles and bring to a boil. Add the noodles and toss to separate. Cook until the noodles is al dente, tender but firm.
2. Drain well. Rinse with cold water, drain again and mix with sesame oil.
3. In a heavy-bottomed pan or wok, heat the 3 tablespoons of peanut oil over medium to high heat. Add the noodle. Spread them quickly around the edge of the pan and cook without stirring until they are golden brown at the bottom. It takes between 5 and 8 minutes.
4. Turn it over and brown the other side.
5. Remove from the wok and the plate.
6. Stay warm while you prepare other ingredients for your meal.
Serving Suggestion: Serve the Pan-Fried Noodles with beef and broccoli stir fry.
Variation Tip: When the noodles are done, add 2 teaspoons of soy sauce and spicy chili sauce, to taste.
Nutritional Information Per Serving:
Calories 395 | Fat 17.8g |Sodium 10mg | Carbs 50g | Fiber 2.3g | Sugar 0.8g | Protein 9.1g

Stir-fried Chicken Lo Mein with Veggies

Prep Time: 15 minutes.
Cook Time: 05 minutes.
Serves: 4
Ingredients:
- ½-pound chicken breast (boneless, skinless)

For the Marinade
- 2 teaspoons light soy sauce
- 1 teaspoon rice wine (or dry sherry)
- ¼ teaspoon sesame seed oil
- 1 teaspoon corn-starch

For the Sauce
- ¾ cup chicken broth
- 2 tablespoons plus 1 teaspoon oyster sauce
- ¾ teaspoon sugar

Other Stir-Fry Ingredients
- ½-pound Chinese noodles (thin or thick noodles are fine)
- 1 cup carrots (shredded; about 1 carrot)
- 1 (8-ounce) can straw mushrooms
- 3 tablespoons vegetable oil (or peanut oil for stir-frying, or as needed)
- 1 teaspoon garlic (chopped)
- ¼ teaspoon salt (plus more, to taste)
- Freshly ground black pepper (to taste)

Preparation:
1. Cut the chicken into thin strips about 2 cm long.
2. In a medium bowl, add light soy sauce, rice wine or dry sherry, sesame oil and corn-starch. Marinate the chicken for 20 minutes.
3. While the chicken marinates, transfer the sauce ingredients to a bowl and set aside.
4. Cook the noodles in boiling water until al dente (tender but still firm). It takes about 3 minutes for fresh noodles and 4-5 minutes for dry noodles.
5. Drain, rinse with cold water and rinse again.
6. Cut the carrot into thin strips to match the chicken.
7. Rinse the straw mushrooms under running water to remove any "tin taste". Drain well
8. Heat 1 tablespoon of oil over medium to high heat. Add the garlic and cook for a few seconds until it is aromatic. Cook the garlic in a wok. Add the chicken and cook until it changes color and is 80 percent ready. (If you need more oil, try adding 1 tablespoon of water. Remove the chicken and clean the wok.
9. Heat 2 tablespoons of oil and salt in a wok. Add the carrots and mushrooms. Fry for 1 minute.
10. Then add the chicken and the noodles and mix with the other ingredients.
11. Put the sauce in the wok and mix well.
12. Cook for another 2 minutes. Season to taste and season with salt or pepper.
13. Chicken Lo Mein fried in a wok.
Serving Suggestion: Serve with chili garlic sauce.
Variation Tip: Use tofu instead of chicken.
Nutritional Information Per Serving:
Calories 238 | Fat 14.3g |Sodium 2789mg | Carbs 17.5g | Fiber 2.3g | Sugar 7.2g | Protein 17.8g

Noodles with Beans Sauce

Prep Time: 40 minutes.
Cook Time: 20 minutes.
Serves: 4
Ingredients:
- 2 tablespoons vegetable oil
- 3 spring onions, finely chopped
- 1 chili pepper, remove seed and finely chopped
- 2 tablespoons shallots, finely chopped
- 300g beef mince
- 6 pieces of extra-firm tofu, about 1 block, finely chopped
- 2 tablespoons sweet bean sauce
- 3 tablespoons chili bean sauce
- 1 bowl of edamame beans
- ½ cup cold water, divided
- 2 tablespoons light soy sauce
- ½ tablespoon dark soy sauce
- 2 teaspoons sugar
- 2 teaspoons corn flour
- 1 carrot, julienned
- 120g bean sprouts
- 400g noodles
- 1 teaspoon sesame oil

Preparation:
1. Heat 2 tablespoons of oil in a wok and brown the spring onions, chili and shallots until tender.
2. Leave the stove on full power and add the ground beef and fry until cooked through. Add extra firm tofu and fry another 3-4 minutes.
3. Add the sweet bean sauce and chili bean sauce. Fry for a few more minutes and add the edamame beans, 2 teaspoons of water, light soy sauce, dark soy sauce and sugar. Mix evenly.
4. Mix the corn flour with 2 tablespoons of cold water and mix evenly. Cook a few more minutes; the sauce should be thick and almost dry.
5. Bring the water to a boil in a large saucepan and blanch the carrots and bean sprouts.
6. Use the same water to cook the noodles. When the noodles are cooked, cool them in the rest of the cold water and pour some sesame oil over the noodles to prevent them from sticking.

7. Put the noodles, carrots and bean sprouts in a bowl and pour the sauce over it.

8. Serve and enjoy.

Serving Suggestion: Serve with chili garlic sauce.

Variation Tip: You can use pork mince.

Nutritional Information Per Serving:

Calories 664 | Fat 23.8g |Sodium 3178mg | Carbs 99.5g | Fiber 6.3g | Sugar 12.4g | Protein 26.7g

Chicken and Chow Mein Noodles

Prep Time: 15 minutes
Cook Time: 6minutes
Servings: 3
Ingredients:
For sauce:
- 1½ tablespoons Chinese cooking wine
- 2 teaspoons corn flour
- 1½ tablespoons soy sauce
- 1½ tablespoons oyster sauce
- ½ teaspoon sesame oil
- 2 teaspoons sugar
- Freshly ground white pepper, to taste

For chicken & noodles:
- 6 ounces chicken breast, sliced thinly
- 6 ounces chow Mein noodles
- 1½ tablespoons peanut oil
- 2 garlic cloves, chopped finely
- 4 cups green cabbage, shredded finely
- 1 carrot, peeled and julienned
- 3 scallions (white and green parts separated), cut into 2-inch pieces
- 1½ cups bean sprouts
- ¼ cup water

Preparation:
1. For sauce: in a bowl, add all sauce ingredients and beat until well combined.
2. In a large bowl, add 1 tablespoon of sauce and chicken slices and toss to coat well.
3. Set aside to marinate for about 10 minutes.
4. In a pan of boiling water, cook the noodles for about 1 minute or according to the package's instructions.
5. Drain the noodles well and set aside.
6. In a large skillet, heat the oil over high heat and sauté the garlic for about 10 seconds.
7. Add the chicken slices and stir fry for about 1 minute.
8. Add the cabbage, carrot and white part of scallions and stir fry for about 1½ minutes.
9. Add the noodles, sauce and water and stir fry for about 1 minute.
10. Add the bean sprouts and scallion greens and cook for about 30 seconds, tossing frequently.

11. Serve immediately.

Serving Suggestions: Serve with the garnishing of sesame seeds.

Variation Tip: Dry, thin noodles are a good choice for chow Mein.

Nutritional Information per Serving:

Calories: 523 | Fat: 27g|Sat Fat: 3.9g|Carbohydrates: 50.5g|Fiber: 5.7g|Sugar: 7.4g|Protein: 23g

Scrumptious Sriracha Chicken Noodles

Prep Time: 05 minutes.
Cook Time: 10 minutes.
Serves: 10
Ingredients:
- ⅔ cup low-sodium soy sauce
- 3 tablespoons honey
- 1 tablespoon Sriracha or chili sauce
- 1 tablespoon lime zest
- 1 tablespoon vegetable oil
- 2 chicken breasts, cut into 1" pieces
- 1 head of broccoli, cut into small florets
- 2 cloves garlic, minced
- 1 tablespoon freshly grated ginger
- ¼ cup sliced green onions
- 12 ounces cooked rice or Udon noodles
- Lime wedges, for serving
- Salt and pepper, to taste
- Cilantro, finely chopped for garnish

Preparation:
1. Make salsa. In a medium bowl, combine soy sauce, honey, sriracha and lime zest.
2. Meanwhile, heat the oil in a large skillet over medium heat. Season the chicken with salt and pepper, then place it in a hot pan. Fry until golden brown on all sides and almost cooked through, about 6 to 8 minutes.
3. Add the broccoli and stir in the chicken until the broccoli begins to turn light green and tender. Add the garlic and ginger and cook until fragrant, about 1 minute.
4. Add the sauce and bring to a boil. Reduce the sauce a little and simmer until the chicken is cooked through and the broccoli is tender. Add the pasta and stir until completely combined.
5. Add the spring onions and cilantro. Serve immediately with lime wedges.

Serving Suggestion: Serve with chili garlic sauce.

Variation Tip: Use cauliflower.

Nutritional Information Per Serving:

Calories 561 | Fat 9.4g |Sodium 2278mg | Carbs 87.5g | Fiber 2.3g | Sugar 16.2g | Protein 32.7g

Shrimp Lo Mein with Vegetables

Prep Time: 15 minutes
Cook Time: 22 minutes
Servings: 4
Ingredients:
For sauce:
- 1 packet chicken bouillon mix
- 1¾ cups hot water
- ¼ cup plus 2 tablespoons oyster sauce
- 3 tablespoons low-sodium soy sauce
- 1 tablespoon Sriracha chili sauce
- 1 tablespoon sesame oil

For Lo Mein:
- 8 ounces dried Chinese egg noodles
- 2 tablespoons vegetable oil, divided
- 1 small bunch scallion, sliced and divided
- 1 tablespoon garlic, minced and divided
- 2 teaspoons fresh ginger, minced and divided
- 1-pound small shrimp, peeled and deveined
- 2 celery stalks, sliced thinly
- 1 large carrot, peeled and shredded
- 1 cup white button mushrooms, sliced thinly
- ¼ head Napa cabbage, shredded finely
- 2 tablespoons corn-starch
- 2 tablespoons cold water

Preparation:
1. For sauce: in a bowl, dissolve the bouillon mix in hot water.
2. Add the remaining ingredients and stir to combine.
3. For lo Mein: in a large pan of salted boiling water, cook the noodles for about 8-10 minutes.
4. Drain the noodles and set aside.
5. In a skillet, heat 1 tablespoon of oil over high heat and sauté half of the scallion, garlic and ginger for about 30 seconds.
6. Add the shrimp and stir fry for about 2 minutes.
7. With a slotted spoon, transfer the shrimp mixture into a bowl. Set aside.
8. In the same skillet, heat the remaining oil over high heat and sauté the remaining scallion, garlic and ginger for about 30 seconds.
9. Add the celery, carrots, mushrooms and cabbage and sauté for about 4-5 minutes.
10. Meanwhile, dissolve the corn-starch in cold water.
11. Add the corn-starch mixture into the pan of veggie mixture and stir to combine.
12. Stir in the sauce and bring to a gentle simmer.
13. Add the cooked shrimp mixture and noodles and toss to coat well.
14. Serve hot.
Serving Suggestions: Serve with a topping of roasted peanuts.

Variation Tip: For a spicy kick, try to add a little sriracha.
Nutritional Information per Serving:
Calories: 361 | Fat: 13.5g|Sat Fat: 2.7g|Carbohydrates: 28.9g|Fiber: 3g|Sugar: 3.9g|Protein: 30.9g

Shaanxi Biang Biang Mian

Prep Time: 20 minutes
Cook Time: 57 minutes
Servings: 4
Ingredients:
For chili oil:
- 1 bulb garlic, grated
- 2 tablespoons soy sauce
- 2 cups peanut oil
- ½ cup Chinese chili powder
- ¼ cup white sesame seeds
- 1 teaspoon ground cumin
- 1 teaspoon ground coriander
- 2 dried bay leaves
- 2-star anises
- 1-2 tablespoons ground Sichuan peppercorns

For seasoned soy sauce:
- ¾ cup soy sauce
- ¼ cup water
- 1 tablespoon light brown sugar
- 2 teaspoon whole Sichuan peppercorn
- 1 star anise
- ½ of cinnamon stick
- 2 whole cloves
- ⅓ cup black vinegar

For tomato sauce:
- 1 tablespoon peanut oil
- 3 tomatoes, chopped
- 3 tablespoons tomato paste

For noodles:
- 7 ounces dried noodles

Preparation:
For chili oil:
1. In a small bowl, mix together the garlic and soy sauce. Set aside.
2. In a large skillet, add the peanut oil, chili powder, sesame seeds, cumin, coriander, bay leaves and star anise over medium-low heat and cook for about 3-4 minutes, stirring frequently.
3. Stir in the ground peppercorn and cook for about 10-20 seconds, stirring continuously.
4. Add the garlic mixture and gently stir to combine.
5. Remove from the heat and transfer the chili oi into a heatproof bowl.
6. Set aside to cool.
7. After cooling, discard the bay leaves and star anise.
8. Set aside for about 2 hours before using.

For seasoned soy sauce:
9. In a small saucepan, add all ingredients except for vinegar over medium-low heat and bring to a gentle simmer.
10. Reduce the heat to low and let simmer for about 15 minutes.
11. Remove from the heat and strain the seasoned soy sauce into a heatproof bowl.
12. Add the black vinegar and mix well.
13. Set aside to cool before using.
For tomato sauce:
14. In a medium skillet, heat the oil over medium heat and cook the tomato and tomato paste for about 5-7 minutes, crushing the tomatoes with the back of the spoon.
15. Transfer the tomato sauce into a bowl and set aside.
16. In a large pan of boiling water, cook the noodles for about 8-10 minutes.
17. Drain the noodles and rinse under cold running water.
18. Again, drain the noodles and transfer into a bowl.
19. Add the chili oil, tomato sauce and seasoned soy sauce and toss to coat well.
20. Serve immediately.
Serving Suggestions: Serve with the garnishing of scallion.
Variation Tip: Use wide-sized noodles for this recipe.
Nutritional Information per Serving:
Calories: 679 | Fat: 44.6g|Sat Fat: 6.9g|Carbohydrates: 51.7g|Fiber: 16g|Sugar: 8.7g|Protein: 3.1g

Spiced Chow Mein with Veggies

Prep Time: 15 minutes
Cook Time: 23 minutes
Servings: 4
Ingredients:
• 10½ ounces egg noodles
• 1 tablespoon vegetable oil
• 2 cups mushrooms, sliced thinly
• 1 red bell pepper, seeded and sliced thinly
• 3 scallions, chopped finely
• 2 teaspoons fresh ginger, minced
• 3 garlic cloves, chopped finely
• 10 baby corn, halved lengthwise
• 2 cups broccolini, halved lengthwise
• 1 cup sugar snap peas, halved lengthwise
• 2 cups fresh baby spinach
• 2-3 tablespoons soy sauce
• 2 tablespoons oyster sauce
• 1 teaspoon sesame oil
• 1 tablespoon fresh lemon juice
Preparation:
1. In a large pan of salted boiling water, cook the noodles for about 8-10 minutes.
2. Drain the noodles and set aside.

3. In a skillet, heat the vegetable oil over medium heat and stir fry the mushrooms, bell peppers, scallions, ginger and garlic for about 5 minutes.
4. Add the corn, broccolini and sugar snap beans and stir fry for about 5 minutes.
5. Add the spinach, soy sauce, oyster sauce and sesame oil and stir fry for about 2 minutes.
6. Add the cooked noodles and lemon juice and toss to combine.
7. Serve hot.
Serving Suggestions: Serve with the topping of a little chili oil.
Variation Tip: Feel free to use veggies of your choice.
Nutritional Information per Serving:
Calories: 214 | Fat: 6.7g|Sat Fat: 1.2g|Carbohydrates: 32.9g|Fiber: 4.6g|Sugar: 6g|Protein: 8.3g

Sesame Noodles with Scallions

Prep Time: 10 minutes
Cook Time: 10 minutes
Servings: 4
Ingredients:
• 1-pound uncooked noodles
• ¼ cup low-sodium soy sauce
• 2 tablespoons rice vinegar
• 1 tablespoon sesame oil, toasted
• ½ teaspoon chili garlic sauce
• 1 teaspoon ground ginger
• ½ teaspoon garlic powder
• ¼ teaspoon freshly ground black pepper
• ½ cup scallions, sliced
• 1 teaspoon sesame seeds, toasted
Preparation:
1. In a large pan of salted boiling water, cook the noodles for about 8-10 minutes.
2. Meanwhile, in a bowl, add the soy sauce, vinegar, sesame oil, chili garlic sauce, ground ginger, garlic powder and black pepper and beat until well combined.
3. Drain the noodles and rinse under cold running water.
4. Again, drain the noodles and transfer into a bowl.
5. Add the vinegar mixture and scallions toss to coat well.
6. Garnish with sesame seeds and serve.
Serving Suggestions: Serve with the garnishing of fresh ginger slices.
Variation Tip: Feel free to use seasoning according to your taste buds.
Nutritional Information per Serving:
Calories: 378 | Fat: 6.4g|Sat Fat: 0.9g|Carbohydrates: 64.8g|Fiber: 0.5g|Sugar: 1.4g|Protein: 14.3g

Beef Noodles in Chili Sauce

Prep Time: 15 minutes
Cook Time: 13 minutes
Servings: 6
Ingredients:
For noodles:
• 1 pound wheat-flour noodles
• 1 teaspoon sesame oil, toasted
For beef mixture:
• 2 tablespoons peanut oil
• 3 red Fresno chiles, stemmed, seeded and chopped finely
• 1 tablespoon fresh ginger root, grated
• 2 garlic cloves, minced
• 9 ounces ground beef
• ½ cup cornichons, chopped finely
• 1 tablespoon Chinese sesame paste
• 1 tablespoon rice wine
• 1 tablespoon black rice vinegar
• 1 tablespoon light soy sauce
• 1 teaspoon ground Sichuan peppercorns
• Freshly ground white pepper, to taste
For garnishing:
• 3 red Fresno chiles, stemmed, seeded and finely diced
• ¼ cup sesame oil, toasted
• ¼ cup chili oil
• ¼ cup light soy sauce
• 1 tablespoon ground Sichuan peppercorns
• 3-4 cups boiling low-sodium chicken broth
• 2 large scallions, chopped
Preparation:
For noodles:
1. In a large pan of salted boiling water, cook the noodles for about 4 minutes.
2. Drain the noodles and rinse under cold running water.
3. Again, drain the noodles and transfer into a bowl.
4. Add the sesame oil and toss to coat.
For beef mixture:
5. In a skillet, heat the oil over high heat and stir fry the chiles, ginger, and garlic for about 30 seconds.
6. Add the ground beef and cook for about 2-3 minutes, breaking up the meat with a spatula.
7. Stir in the cornichons, sesame paste, wine, vinegar, soy sauce and peppercorns and cook for about 4-5 minutes.
8. Stir in the white pepper and remove from the heat.
For garnishing:
9. In a small bowl, mix together the chiles, sesame oil, chili oil, soy sauce and peppercorns.
10. Divide the noodles into serving bowls and pour in the hot broth.

11. Top with beef mixture, scallion and oil mixture and serve.
Serving Suggestions: Serve with the garnishing of peanuts.
Variation Tip: You can adjust the spice level by adding more or less chili oil.
Nutritional Information per Serving:
Calories: 597 | Fat: 29.7g|Sat Fat: 5.9g|Carbohydrates: 56.4g|Fiber: 5.9g|Sugar: 7g|Protein: 28.7g

Chicken Dragon Noodles

Prep Time: 15 minutes.
Cook Time: 25 minutes.
Serves: 4
Ingredients:
For the noodles
• 1 tablespoon vegetable oil
• 3 boneless skinless chicken breasts
• 2 teaspoons garlic powder
• 1 teaspoon cayenne
• Kosher salt
• Freshly ground black pepper
• 3 cloves garlic, minced
• ¼ cup thinly sliced green onions
• 1 red bell pepper, chopped
• 1 large carrot, cut into matchsticks
• 1 large zucchini, cut into half moons
• 12 ounces cooked lo Mein noodles
• Freshly chopped cilantro, for garnish
For the sauce
• ⅓ cup low-sodium soy sauce
• Juice of ½ lime
• 2 tablespoons chili garlic sauce (or Sriracha)
• 1 tablespoon creamy peanut butter
• 2 tablespoons low-sodium chicken broth
Preparation:
1. In a large skillet, heat the oil over medium heat. Add the chicken and season with garlic powder, cayenne pepper, salt, and ground black pepper. Bake for 8 minutes until golden, then flip the other side and season and cook for another 8 minutes. Let stand 10 minutes, then cut into small pieces.
2. Add the garlic and spring onions to the pan and cook for 1 minute until fragrant. Add the bell peppers, carrots and zucchini and cook for another 6 minutes until tender.
3. Meanwhile, prepare the sauce: Combine the soy sauce, lemon juice, chili garlic sauce, peanut butter and chicken broth in a bowl.
4. Add the cooked chicken to the vegetables and pour the sauce over it. Simmer for 2 minutes, then add the cooked noodles and mix gently.

5. Garnish with cilantro and serve.
Serving Suggestion: Serve with chili garlic sauce.
Variation Tip: Use turkey breast.
Nutritional Information Per Serving:
Calories 480 | Fat 8.1g |Sodium 1178mg | Carbs 78.5g | Fiber 6.3g | Sugar 14.2g | Protein 19.7g

Calamari and Noodles

Prep Time: 15 minutes
Cook Time: 2 minutes
Servings: 4
Ingredients:
For noodles:
• 8 ounces vermicelli noodles
• 2 tablespoons peanut oil
For dressing:
• 1 tablespoon fresh ginger, grated finely
• 3-4 tablespoons fresh grapefruit juice
• 1 tablespoon fresh lemon juice
• 1-2 tablespoons Sriracha
• 1 tablespoon honey
• 1 tablespoon light brown sugar
• 1 Serrano chile, sliced into thin rings
For calamari:
• 1 teaspoon Chinese five-spice powder
• 1 teaspoon sea salt
• 1 teaspoon ground white pepper
• 3 large egg yolks, beaten
• 2 tablespoons potato starch
• 1 pound fresh squid tubes, cleaned and sliced into rings
• 1-2 cups vegetable oil
Preparation:
For the noodles:
1. In a large bowl, add the noodles and top with the boiling water.
2. Set aside for about 4 minutes.
3. Drain the noodles and rinse under cold running water.
4. Again, drain the noodles and transfer into a bowl.
5. Add the oil and toss to coat well. Set aside.
For the dressing
6. In a bowl, add all ingredients except for chile and eat until well combined.
7. Add the chile and stir to combine. Set aside.
For the calamari:
8. In a small bowl, add the five-spice powder, salt and white pepper and mix well. Set aside.
9. In another bowl, add the egg yolks and potato starch and beat until well combined.
10. Dip the calamari rings into the starch mixture evenly over high heat and fry the calamari rings for about 2 minutes, stirring frequently.

11. With a slotted spoon, place the calamari rings onto a paper towel-lined plate to drain.
12. Sprinkle the hot calamari rings with spice mixture.
13. Divide the noodles into 4 shallow bowls and drizzle with ⅔ of the dressing.
14. Top each bowl with calamari and then drizzle with the remaining dressing.
15. Serve hot.
Serving Suggestions: Serve with the garnishing of fresh herbs.
Variation Tip: Fresh squid should look shiny and plump, not deflated.
Nutritional Information per Serving:
Calories: 931 | Fat: 66.3g|Sat Fat: 47.3g|Carbohydrates: 64g|Fiber: 2.4g|Sugar: 7.5g|Protein: 23g

Chicken Noodles with Peanuts

Prep Time: 05 minutes.
Cook Time: 15 minutes.
Serves: 10
Ingredients:
• 1 (12-oz.) package No Yolks Extra Broad Noodles
• 2 cups shredded chicken, cooked
• 1 red bell pepper, thinly sliced
• 1 yellow bell pepper, thinly sliced
• 1 cucumber, thinly sliced
• 1 carrot, shredded
• 1 tablespoon thinly sliced green onions
• 2 tablespoons chopped peanuts
• 2 teaspoons sesame seeds
Dressing
• ½ cup creamy peanut butter
• Juice of 2 limes
• ¼ cup low-sodium soy sauce
• 3 tablespoons rice vinegar
• 2 tablespoons grated fresh ginger
• 1 tablespoon sesame oil
• 1 clove garlic, minced
• 1 teaspoon crushed red pepper flakes
Preparation:
1. Cook the noodles according to package directions, then drain.
2. Combine all dressing ingredients in a medium bowl.
3. In a large bowl, combine cooked chicken, peppers, cucumber, carrots, and noodles.
4. Pour dressing over salad and toss until completely covered.
5. Garnish with spring onions, peanuts and sesame seeds.
Serving Suggestion: Serve with chili garlic sauce.
Variation Tip: Use turkey instead of chicken.
Nutritional Information Per Serving:
Calories 480 | Fat 8.1g |Sodium 1178mg | Carbs 78.5g | Fiber 6.3g | Sugar 14.2g | Protein 19.7g

Fried Rice with Chicken and Peas

Prep Time: 15 minutes
Cook Time: 13 minutes
Servings: 4
Ingredients:
• 2 eggs
• 1-2 tablespoons oyster sauce
• Salt, to taste
• 4 tablespoons vegetable oil, divided
• 1 medium onion, chopped
• ½ cup green peas
• 4 cups cooked rice, cooled
• 1-2 tablespoons soy sauce
• Freshly ground black pepper, to taste
• 8 ounces cooked chicken, chopped
• 1 scallion, chopped
Preparation:
1. In a small bowl, add the eggs, dash of oyster sauce and pinch of salt and beat until well combined. Set aside.
2. In a skillet, heat 1 tablespoon of oil over medium-high heat and cook the egg mixture for about 2-3 minutes, stirring continuously.
3. Transfer the scrambled eggs onto a plate and set aside.
4. With paper towels, wipe out the skillet.
5. In the same skillet, heat 1 tablespoon of oil over high heat and sauté the onion for about 2-3 minutes.
6. Transfer the onion onto a plate.
7. In the same skillet, heat 1 tablespoon of oil over high heat and sauté the green peas for about 1-2 minutes.
8. Transfer the peas onto a plate.
9. In the same skillet, heat the remaining oil over medium heat and sauté the cooked rice for about 1-2 minutes.
10. Stir in the oyster sauce, soy sauce, salt and black pepper and stir fry for about 1 minute.
11. Stir in the chicken, eggs, onion and green peas and stir fry for about 1-2 minutes.
12. Stir in the scallion and remove from the heat.
13. Serve hot.
Serving Suggestions: Serve with your favorite dipping sauce.
Variation Tip: Use day-old cooked cold white rice.
Nutritional Information per Serving:
Calories: 449 | Fat: 18g|Sat Fat: 3.9g|Carbohydrates: 45.5g|Fiber: 2.3g|Sugar: 2.6g|Protein: 24.6g

Fried Rice with Peas and Pork

Prep Time: 05 minutes plus 30 minutes for marinating.
Cook Time: 10 minutes.
Serves: 8
Ingredients:
• 2 (4-ounce) boned center-cut loin pork chops
• 1 tablespoon low-sodium soy sauce
• 1 tablespoon dry sherry
• 2 large egg whites
• 1 large egg
• Cooking spray
• 2 teaspoons dark sesame oil, divided
• 2 cups vertically sliced onion
• 2 cups snow peas
• 2 cups sliced mushrooms
• 1 tablespoon minced peeled fresh ginger
• 2 garlic cloves, minced
• 4 cups cooked long-grain rice, chilled
• ¼ teaspoon salt
• ⅓ cup chopped green onions
Preparation:
1. Cut the fat off the pork chops; Cut the pork into 2 ¼-inch strips. Combine pork, soy sauce and sherry; Cover and marinate in the refrigerator for 30 minutes. Flow out; discard the sherry mixture.
2. Combine egg whites and egg in medium bowl; Mix well with a whisk. Place a large non-stick skillet or wok covered with cooking spray over medium-high heat until heated through. Add the egg mixture; Cook for 2 minutes or until the egg is set. Remove the egg mixture from the pan.
3. Add ½ teaspoon of oil to the pan. Add the pork. Fry for 2 minutes or until cooked through. Remove the pork from the pan; Keep warm. Add ½ teaspoon of oil to the pan. Add onion and sliced peas; Fry for 2 minutes. Add mushrooms, ginger and garlic; Fry for 1 minute. Remove the onion mixture from the pan and keep warm.
4. Put 1 teaspoon of oil in the pan; Add the rice and cook for 1 minute without stirring. Add the egg mixture, pork, onions and salt mixture and sauté for 1 minute or until heated through. Sprinkle each serving with about 1 tablespoon of green onions.
Serving Suggestion: Serve with chili garlic sauce.
Variation Tip: Use beef.
Nutritional Information Per Serving:
Calories 345 | Fat 6.4g |Sodium 238mg | Carbs 50.5g | Fiber 3.7g | Sugar 16.2g | Protein 18.7g

Peppered Fried Brown Rice with Almonds

Prep Time: 05 minutes.
Cook Time: 10 minutes.
Serves: 4
Ingredients:
• 1 tablespoon peanut oil
• ½ cup thinly sliced onion
• 1 teaspoon minced garlic
• 1 ½ cups sliced red bell pepper
• ¼ cup sliced almonds
• 1 (8. 8-ounce) pouch precooked brown rice
• 1 tablespoon fresh lime juice
• 2 teaspoons yellow curry paste
• ¼ cup cilantro leaves
• ¼ teaspoon salt
Preparation:
1. Heat a large wok or skillet over medium heat. Add the oil; Whirlpool. Add the onion and garlic; Fry for 1 minute.
2. Add peppers and nuts; Fry for 2 minutes. Add the rice. Fry for 1 minute.
3. Add the lime juice, curry paste, cilantro and salt.
Serving Suggestion: Serve with chili garlic sauce.
Variation Tip: Use mushroom & pine nut.
Nutritional Information Per Serving:
Calories 169 | Fat 7.4g |Sodium 221mg | Carbs 27.5g | Fiber 2.3g | Sugar 16.2g | Protein 4g

Fried Zucchini and Brown Rice with Walnuts

Prep Time: 05 minutes.
Cook Time: 10 minutes.
Serves: 4
Ingredients:
• 1 tablespoon peanut oil
• ½ cup thinly sliced onion
• 1 teaspoon minced garlic
• 1 ½ cups sliced zucchini
• ¼ cup chopped walnuts

• 1 (8. 8-ounce) pouch precooked brown rice (such as Uncle Ben's)
• 2 tablespoons white wine vinegar
• 2 teaspoons Dijon mustard
• ¼ teaspoon salt
Preparation:
1. Heat a wok or skillet over medium-high heat. Add peanut oil; Whirlpool. Add the onion and garlic; Fry for 1 minute. Add zucchini and walnuts; Fry for 2 minutes.
2. Add the rice. Fry for 1 minute. Add the vinegar, Dijon mustard and salt.
Serving Suggestion: Serve with chili garlic sauce.
Variation Tip: Use cauliflower.
Nutritional Information Per Serving:
Calories 177 | Fat 9.4g |Sodium 191mg | Carbs 7.5g | Fiber 2.3g | Sugar 16.2g | Protein 32.7g

Fried Rice with Veggies

Prep Time: 05 minutes.
Cook Time: 10 minutes.
Serves:6
Ingredients:
• 1 egg
• ⅛ teaspoon salt
• 1 tablespoon low-sodium soy sauce
• 1 teaspoon peanut oil
• ½ teaspoon brown sugar
• Vegetable cooking spray
• 1 cup sliced celery
• ½ cup sliced onion, cut in half
• 1 cup sliced fresh mushrooms
• 1 (6-ounce) package smoked tofu, crumbled
• 2 cloves garlic, crushed
• 3 cups cooked long-grain rice (cooked without salt or fat)
• 1 cup frozen English peas, thawed
Preparation:
1. Combine egg and salt and beat until fluffy with a whisk. Put aside. Combine soy sauce, oil and sugar. Put aside.
2. Brush a wok with cooking spray. Heat over medium heat (375 °) until hot. Add celery and onion; Fry for 2 minutes. Add mushrooms, tofu and garlic; Fry for 1 minute.
3. Slide the vegetable mixture down the sides of the wok and form a hole in the center. Pour the egg mixture into the well and sauté until firm. Add the rice and brown for 1 minute. Add soy sauce mixture and peas; Fry for 2 minutes. Use immediately.
Serving Suggestion: Serve with chili garlic sauce.
Variation Tip: Use choice of vegetables.
Nutritional Information Per Serving:
Calories 202 | Fat 2g |Sodium 204mg | Carbs 31.5g | Fiber 2.3g | Sugar 16.2g | Protein 12.7g

Egg-fried rice

Prep Time: 10 minutes.
Cook Time: 10 minutes.
Serves: 4
Ingredients:
- 250g long grain rice
- 3 tablespoons vegetable oil
- 1 onion, finely chopped
- 4 eggs, beaten
- 2 spring onions, sliced, to serve

Preparation:
1. Cook rice according to package directions, drain, steam dry and set aside.
2. Heat 2 tablespoons of oil in a large wok over high heat, then add the onion and sauté for about 5 minutes until lightly browned. Add the rice, stir and roast for about 3 minutes, then place on the edge of the pan.
3. Add the rest of the oil, then pour in the egg mixture. Let it boil a little, then mix with the rice; Stir vigorously to coat the grains or, if you prefer thicker egg, let it sit a little longer before breaking and stirring. Transfer to a serving bowl and spread over the chives to serve.
Serving Suggestion: Serve the egg fried rice with chili garlic sauce.
Variation Tip: Use green peas and carrot if you like.
Nutritional Information Per Serving:
Calories 395 | Fat 14g |Sodium 67mg | Carbs 53.4g | Fiber 1.3g | Sugar 1.8g | Protein 10.4g

Fried Rice with Scrambled Eggs

Prep Time: 10 minutes
Cook Time: 7 minutes
Servings: 4
Ingredients:
- 2 large eggs
- 1 teaspoon salt
- Freshly ground black pepper, to taste

- 3 tablespoons canola oil, divided
- 4 cups cooked rice, cooled
- 1-2 tablespoons light soy sauce
- 1-2 scallions, chopped

Preparation:
1. In a bowl, add the eggs, salt, and black pepper and beat lightly.
2. In a skillet, heat 1 tablespoon of the oil over medium-high heat and cook the egg mixture for about 2-3 minutes, stirring continuously.
3. Transfer the scrambled eggs onto a plate and set aside.
4. With paper towels, wipe out the skillet.
5. In the same skillet, heat the remaining oil over medium heat and stir-fry the cooked rice for about 1-2 minutes.
6. Add the soy sauce and stir to combine.
7. Add the scrambled egg and stir to combine.
8. Stir in the scallion and remove from the heat.
9. Serve hot.
Serving Suggestions: Hot and sour soup will go great with this rice.
Variation Tip: Use medium to long grain rice, not short grain one.
Nutritional Information per Serving:
Calories: 314 | Fat: 13.4g|Sat Fat: 1.7g|Carbohydrates: 40.2g|Fiber: 0.7g|Sugar: 0.5g|Protein: 7.3g

Awesome Vegetable Fried Rice

Prep Time: 15 minutes
Cook Time: 6 minutes
Servings: 4
Ingredients:
- 4 tablespoons butter
- ½ cup onion, cut into 1-inch cubes
- 2 teaspoons garlic, chopped
- ¼ cup carrots, peeled and chopped
- ¼ cup peas
- 2 eggs, beaten
- 4 cups cooked rice
- 1 tablespoon sesame oil, toasted
- 1 tablespoon soy sauce
- Salt, to taste
- ½ teaspoon ground white pepper

Preparation:
1. In a skillet, melt butter over medium heat and stir fry onion and garlic for about 1 minute.
2. Add carrots and peas and stir fry for about 1 minute.

3. With the spatula, push the vegetables on one side of skillet.
4. Add the beaten eggs and cook for about 2 minutes, stirring continuously.
5. Now mix the eggs with vegetables.
6. Add the cooked rice, salt, white pepper powder, soy sauce, sesame oil and cook for about 1-2 minutes, tossing frequently.
7. Serve hot.
Serving Suggestions: Serve alongside the cooked basil chicken.
Variation Tip: You can use frozen vegetables too.
Nutritional Information per Serving:
Calories: 369 | Fat: 17.6g|Sat Fat: 8.6g|Carbohydrates: 43.8g|Fiber: 1.7g|Sugar: 1.8g|Protein: 7.8g

Authentic Yangchow Fried Rice

Prep Time: 15 minutes
Cook Time: 13 minutes
Servings: 6
Ingredients:
• 4 ounces frozen medium shrimp, thawed, peeled and deveined
• ½ teaspoon corn-starch
• Salt and freshly ground black pepper, to taste
• 5 tablespoons canola oil
• 6 ounces roast pork, chopped
• 1 medium yellow onion, chopped
• ½ cup frozen peas, thawed
• 4 cups cooked rice, cooled
• 3 large eggs, beaten lightly
Preparation:
1. In a bowl, add the shrimp, corn-starch, salt and black pepper and toss to coat well.
2. In a skillet, heat 1 tablespoon of oil over medium heat and stir fry the shrimp for about 2 minutes.
3. Push the shrimp up to the side of skillet and stir fry the pork for about 1-2 minutes.
4. Transfer the shrimp and pork onto a plate.
5. In the same skillet, heat 2 tablespoons of oil over medium heat and sauté the onion for about 3-4 minutes.
6. Add the peas and stir fry for about 2 minutes.
7. Transfer the onion and peas onto a plate.
8. In the same skillet, heat the remaining oil over medium heat and stir fry the rice for about 1-2 minutes.
9. Add the beaten egg and cook for about 2 minutes, stirring continuously.
10. Add the shrimp, pork, onion, peas, salt and black pepper and cook for about 1 minute.
11. Serve hot.

Serving Suggestions: Serve with your favorite soup.
Variation Tip: Use a well-seasoned skillet for this recipe.
Nutritional Information per Serving:
Calories: 4143 | Fat: 20.6g|Sat Fat: 1.8g|Carbohydrates: 32.6g|Fiber: 1.5g|Sugar: 1.7g|Protein: 22.4g

Chinese Pearl Balls

Prep Time: 20 minutes
Cook Time: 25 to 35 minutes
Servings: 15
Ingredients:
• ¾ cup glutinous rice, soaked overnight and drained
• 1 pound ground pork
• 2 water chestnuts, minced
• 1 large scallion, minced
• 1 large egg white
• 1 tablespoon light soy sauce
• 1 tablespoon dry sherry
• 1 teaspoon salt
• Freshly ground black pepper, to taste
Preparation:
1. Spread the drained rice onto a baking sheet and set aside.
2. In a large bowl, add the remaining ingredients and mix until well combined.
3. With 1 tablespoon of pork mixture, make small sized balls.
4. Roll the meatballs in the glutinous rice to coat completely.
5. Arrange the balls onto a heatproof plate.
6. Place a large pan of water over medium heat and bring to a boil.
7. Arrange the steamer over water without touching.
8. Now place the plate of balls in the steamer.
9. Cover and steam for about 25-35 minutes or until done completely.
10. Serve warm.
Serving Suggestions: Serve alongside soy sauce.
Variation Tip: Make sure to use glutinous rice in this recipe.
Nutritional Information per Serving:
Calories: 86 | Fat: 1.2g|Sat Fat: 0.4g|Carbohydrates: 9g|Fiber: 0.1g|Sugar: 0.1g|Protein: 9g

Flavorful Lotus Leaf Rice Wraps

Prep Time: 25 minutes plus 25 minutes for marinating.
Cook Time: 35 minutes.
Servings: 8
Ingredients:
• 1 (6-ounce) boneless, skinless chicken breast, cut into small cubes
• 2 tablespoons Chinese rice wine, divided
• 2½ teaspoons corn-starch, divided
• ¼ teaspoon salt
• 1¼ cups glutinous rice, soaked for 1 hour and drained
• 4 dried black mushrooms, soaked in hot water for 20-30 minutes and drained
• 1 tablespoon water
• 1 tablespoon light soy sauce
• 1 teaspoon dark soy sauce
• 2 tablespoons vegetable oil
• 1 garlic clove, chopped
• 2 Chinese sausages, sliced finely
• Freshly ground black pepper, to taste
• ¼ teaspoon sesame oil
• 4 lotus leaves, cut in half, soaked in hot water for 1 hour, drained and dried

Preparation:
1. In a bowl, add chicken cubes, 1 tablespoon of wine, 1 teaspoon of corn-starch and salt and toss to coat well.
2. Refrigerate to marinate for about 20-25 minutes.
3. Line a bamboo steamer with parchment paper and then place the rice.
4. Fill a large skillet with water about halfway.
5. Arrange the steamer over water without touching.
6. Place the skillet over medium heat and bring the water to a boil.
7. Cover the rice and steam for about 20 minutes.
8. Remove the rice from the steamer and set aside, covered to keep warm.

9. Meanwhile, drain the mushrooms and then squeeze out any excess water.
10. Remove the stems of mushrooms and then chop them finely. Set aside.
11. In a small bowl, dissolve the remaining corn-starch in the water.
12. In another small bowl, add the remaining wine and both soy sauces.
13. Add the corn-starch mixture and beat until well combined. Set aside.
For the filling:
14. In a skillet, heat the vegetable oil over medium heat and sauté the garlic for about 30 seconds.
15. Add the chicken cubes and stir fry for about 3-4 minutes.
16. Add the sausages and mushrooms and stir fry for about 1 minute.
17. Add the sauce mixture and stir until well combined.
18. Stir in the black pepper and cook for about 1-2 minutes, stirring continuously.
19. Remove from the heat and stir in the sesame oil.
20. Set aside to cool.
For the wraps:
21. Divide the rice and filling into 8 equal-sized portions.
22. Arrange the lotus leaves onto a smooth surface.
23. Place 1 portion of rice into the center of a lotus leaf and top with the filling mixture.
24. With your hands, shape the rice to forms a ring around the filling.
25. Form a square parcel with the lotus leaf and then tie it with twine.
26. Repeat with the remaining lotus leaves, rice and filling.
27. Arrange the lotus parcels onto a heatproof plate
28. Again, fill the large skillet with water about halfway.
29. Arrange the steamer over water without touching.
30. Now place the plate of wraps in the steamer.
31. Place the skillet over medium heat and bring the water to a boil.
32. Cover the steamer and steam for about 15 minutes.
33. Serve warm.
Serving Suggestions: You can serve these wraps with a little chili oil.
Variation Tip: If you are unable to find lotus leaves, then you can use banana leaves.
Nutritional Information per Serving:
Calories: 242 | Fat: 10g|Sat Fat: 2.6g|Carbohydrates: 26.2g|Fiber: 0.5g|Sugar: 1.2g|Protein: 10.9g

Spicy Kung Pao Chicken

Prep Time: 20 minutes.
Cook Time: 15 minutes.
Serves: 4
Ingredients:
- 1 tablespoon white wine
- 2 tablespoons soy sauce
- 1 teaspoon brown sugar
- 3 medium green onions, finely chopped (white parts only)
- 1-pound skinless, boneless chicken breast, cut into 1-inch pieces
- 1 tablespoon white vinegar
- 2 tablespoons rice vinegar
- 1 tablespoon Asian chili paste (sambal), or more to taste
- 1 tablespoon sesame oil
- 2 tablespoons brown sugar
- 2 teaspoons ketchup
- 2 tablespoons white wine
- 4 cloves garlic, minced
- 1 tablespoon corn-starch
- 2 tablespoons water
- 2 tablespoons peanut oil
- 2 cups cubed zucchini
- 1 cup cubed red bell pepper
- ½ cup chicken broth
- ¼ cup roasted, salted peanuts
- salt and ground black pepper to taste
- ¼ cup chopped green onion tops
- 4 cups cooked white rice

Preparation:
1. Whisk 1 tablespoon of white wine, 1 tablespoon of soy sauce, 1 teaspoon of brown sugar and finely chopped spring onions.
2. Add chicken pieces to coat. Cover and refrigerate for 1 hour.
3. Combine the white vinegar, rice vinegar, 1 tablespoon of soy sauce, sambal chili paste, sesame oil, 2 tablespoons of brown sugar, tomato sauce, 2 tablespoons of white wine and the garlic in a bowl. Hit well; put aside.
4. Combine the corn-starch with cold water in a small bowl.
5. Heat the peanut oil in a non-stick skillet over high heat. Add the chicken. cook and stir until chicken is browned, about 2 minutes.
6. Add zucchini and red pepper; cook for another 2 minutes. Add the chicken broth and stir.
7. Stir in the vinegar mixture; cook and stir until vegetables are tender and chicken is no longer pink in the center, about 2 minutes. Add corn-starch mixture until sauce thickens, about 30 seconds; Remove the stove.
8. Add the peanuts; Season with salt and pepper. Add green onions and stir. Serve over white rice.
Serving Suggestion: Serve with chili garlic sauce.
Variation Tip: Use choice of vegetables.
Nutritional Information Per Serving:
Calories 567 | Fat 12g |Sodium 204mg | Carbs 691.5g | Fiber 3.3g | Sugar 12.2g | Protein 32.7g

Cantonese Steamed Chicken

Prep Time: 15 minutes.
Cook Time: 30 minutes.
Serves: 4
Ingredients:
- 4 to 6 Chinese mushrooms (medium-sized, dried)
- 1 ½ pounds assorted chicken pieces (bone-in)
- ¼ teaspoon salt
- Pepper (to taste)
- 1 ½ tablespoons soy sauce
- 1 tablespoon Chinese rice wine (or dry sherry)
- 1 teaspoon sugar
- 1 teaspoon sesame oil
- 1 ½ tablespoons corn-starch
- 2 slices ginger (shredded)
- 1 green onion (or spring onion, or scallion, diced)

Preparation:
1. Soak the dried mushrooms in a bowl of lukewarm water for 20 minutes or until tender. Squeeze out the excess water, cut the stems of the mushrooms and cut them into thin slices. Keep 1 tablespoon of the mushroom soaking liquid.
2. Use a heavy blade to cut the chicken into bite-sized pieces through the bone. Transfer to a heatproof container and add salt, pepper, soy sauce, rice or sherry wine, sugar, sesame oil, mushroom liquid and corn-starch. Marinate while the water is smoking.
3. Place the container on a rack in a steamer or steamer such as a bamboo steamer in a wok. Place the chicken pieces in the center of the plate and wrap the mushrooms around them. Spread the grated ginger and spring onions on top.
4. Steam the chicken in boiling water for 15 to 20 minutes, making sure it is cooked through. Serve over rice.
Serving Suggestion: Serve with rice.
Variation Tip: Use choice of vegetables.
Nutritional Information Per Serving:
Calories 202 | Fat 2g |Sodium 204mg | Carbs 31.5g | Fiber 2.3g | Sugar 16.2g | Protein 12.7g

Chinese Sweet and Sour Chicken

Prep Time: 10 minutes.
Cook Time: 10 minutes.
Serves: 4
Ingredients:
- 1 pound skinless, boneless chicken breast meat, cubed
- 2 tablespoons vegetable oil
- ½ cup sliced green bell pepper
- ½ cup sliced red bell pepper
- 1 cup carrot strips
- 1 clove garlic, minced
- 1 tablespoon corn-starch
- ¼ cup low sodium soy sauce
- 1 (8 ounce) can pineapple chunks, juice reserved
- 1 tablespoon vinegar
- 1 tablespoon brown sugar
- ½ teaspoon ground ginger

Preparation:
1. Brown the chicken in the oil in a large skillet over medium heat. Add green peppers, red peppers, carrots and garlic and sauté 1 to 2 minutes.
2. In a small bowl, combine and combine the corn-starch and soy sauce; Pour the mixture into the saucepan with the pineapple and the liquid, vinegar, sugar and ginger. Stir and bring to a boil.
Serving Suggestion: Serve with rice or noodles.
Variation Tip: Use honey.
Nutritional Information Per Serving:
Calories 273 | Fat 11g |Sodium 593mg | Carbs 17.5g | Fiber 1.3g | Sugar 10.2g | Protein 26.7g

Spicy Chicken Wings

Prep Time: 05 minutes.
Cook Time: 25 minutes.
Serves: 4
Ingredients:
- 2 pounds chicken wings
- 4 tablespoons white sugar
- 1 cup soy sauce
- ½ cup rice wine
- 6 tablespoons chili garlic sauce
- 4 tablespoons sesame oil
- 4 cloves garlic, minced

- ½ cup water
Preparation:
1. Rinse and dry the chicken wings. Combine the sugar, soy sauce, rice wine, chili garlic sauce, sesame oil and garlic in a large bowl, then add the chicken wings and mix them evenly.
2. Heat a lightly oiled pan over medium heat. Add the chicken wings, sauce and water. Cover and cook until chicken wings are no longer pink on the bone, turning occasionally, about 15 minutes. Remove the lid and continue cooking until the sauce thickens, 5 to 10 minutes.
Serving Suggestion: Serve with noodles.
Variation Tip: Use honey instead of white sugar if you want healthier version.
Nutritional Information Per Serving:
Calories 684 | Fat 30.5g |Sodium 4050mg | Carbs 31.5g | Fiber 0.3g | Sugar 21.2g | Protein 69.7g

Bon Bon Chicken

Prep Time: 10 minutes.
Cook Time: 15 minutes.
Serves: 6
Ingredients:
- 1 cup mayonnaise
- ½ cup sweet chili sauce
- 2 tablespoons Sriracha sauce
- ⅓ cup flour
- 1-pound chicken breast tenderloins, cut into bite-size pieces
- 1 ½ cups panko bread crumbs
- 2 green onions, chopped

Preparation:
1. Whisk mayonnaise, sweet chili sauce and sriracha in a large bowl. Pour ¾ cup of the mixture and set aside.
2. Place the flour in a large resalable plastic bag. Add the chicken, seal the bag and shake to coat. Transfer the coated chicken pieces to the large bowl with the mayo mixture and stir.
3. Place the panko breadcrumbs in another large resalable plastic bag. Add chicken pieces to portioned breadcrumbs, seal and shake to coat.
4. Preheat a deep fryer to 400 ° F (200 ° C).
5. Place as many pieces of chicken as possible in the frying basket without overfilling it. Cook in a hot air fryer for 10 minutes. Flip and cook for another 5 minutes. Repeat with the rest of the chicken.
6. Place the fried chicken in a large bowl and pour the reserved sauce over it. Sprinkle with spring onions and turn to coat. Use immediately.
Serving Suggestion: Serve with chili garlic sauce.
Variation Tip: Use normal bread crumbs.
Nutritional Information Per Serving:
Calories 339 | Fat 17g |Sodium 560mg | Carbs 27g | Fiber 0.3g | Sugar 11.2g | Protein 16.7g

Sesame Marinated Chicken

Prep Time: 15 minutes
Cook Time: 15 minutes
Servings: 5
Ingredients:
For chicken marinade:
• 2 tablespoons water
• 2 tablespoons soy sauce
• 1 tablespoon dry sherry
• Dash of sesame oil
• 2 tablespoons corn-starch
• 2 tablespoons all-purpose flour
• ¼ teaspoon baking soda
• ¼ teaspoon baking powder
• 1 teaspoon canola oil
• 4 (5-ounce) skinless, boneless chicken breast halves, cut into 1-inch cubes
• 2 cups vegetable oil
For sauce:
• 1 cup chicken broth
• ½ cup water
• ¼ cup distilled white vinegar
• 2 tablespoons sesame oil
• 2 tablespoons soy sauce
• 1 teaspoon red chili paste
• 1 cup white sugar
• ¼ cup corn-starch
• 1 garlic clove, minced
• 2 tablespoons sesame seeds, toasted
Preparation:
For chicken marinade:
1. In a large bowl, add all the ingredients except for chicken and vegetable oil and mix until well combined.
2. Add the chicken and coat with mixture generously.
3. Refrigerate, covered for about 20 minutes.
For sauce:
4. In a small pan, mix together all the ingredients except for sesame seed and bring to a boil, stirring continuously.
5. Reduce the heat to low to keep the sauce warm, stirring occasionally.
6. In a large pan, heat the vegetable oil to 375 degrees F and fry the chicken pieces in 2 batches for about 3-5 minutes or until done completely.
7. With a slotted spoon, transfer the chicken pieces onto a paper towels-lined plate to drain.
8. Now, place the chicken pieces onto a serving platter and top with the sauce evenly.
9. Garnish with the sesame seeds and serve.

Serving Suggestions: Serve alongside the hot cooked rice.
Variation Tip: Try to cut chicken into equal=sized cubes.
Nutritional Information per Serving:
Calories: 999 | Fat: 90.1g|Sat Fat: 12.6g|Carbohydrates: 54.1g|Fiber: 0.7g|Sugar: 40g|Protein: 26.9g

Caramelized Chicken Thighs

Prep Time: 10 minutes
Cook Time: 18 to 20 minutes
Servings: 4
Ingredients:
• 1 small yellow onion, minced
• 2 garlic cloves, minced
• 2 tablespoons fresh cilantro, minced
• ⅓ cup ketchup
• ⅓ cup soy sauce
• 2½ tablespoons apple cider vinegar
• 1 tablespoon olive oil
• 1 tablespoon sugar
• 1 teaspoon red pepper flakes, crushed
• Freshly ground black pepper, to taste
• 4 (6-ounce) skinless, boneless chicken thighs
Preparation:
1. In a glass baking dish, add all the ingredients except for chicken thighs and mix well.
2. Add the chicken thighs and coat with the mixture generously.
3. Refrigerate to marinate overnight.
4. Preheat the broiler of oven. Line a large baking sheet with a greased piece of foil.
5. Remove the chicken thighs from bowl, reserving the remaining marinade.
6. Arrange the chicken thighs onto the prepared baking sheet in a single layer and broil for about 5 minutes per side.
7. Meanwhile, transfer the reserved marinade into a small pan over medium heat and cook for about 8-10 minutes.
8. Serve the chicken thighs with the topping of glaze.
Serving Suggestions: Serve with steamed greens.
Variation Tip: Apple cider vinegar can be replaced with lime juice too.
Nutritional Information per Serving:
Calories: 304 | Fat: 9.8g|Sat Fat: 2.8g|Carbohydrates: 12.4g|Fiber: 0.8g|Sugar: 8.9g|Protein: 40g

Sesame Ginger Marinated Chicken

Prep Time: 15 minutes.
Cook Time: 15 minutes.
Serves: 2
Ingredients:
Chicken Marinade:
• 1 ¼ pounds boneless, skinless chicken thighs, cut into 1-inch cubes
• 3 tablespoons sesame oil
• 1 ¼ tablespoons sugar
• 1 tablespoons soy sauce
• ½ teaspoon cracked black pepper
Stir-Fry:
• ½ cup plus 1 tablespoon corn-starch
• Vegetable or peanut oil
• 1 tablespoon minced garlic
• ½ tablespoon minced ginger
• 2 tablespoons Chinese Shaoxing rice wine
• 1 tablespoon hoisin sauce
• 1 tablespoon oyster sauce
• 1 tablespoon low-sodium soy sauce
• ¾ tablespoon honey
• ½ tablespoon sambal chili sauce
• ½ tablespoon Thai chili sauce
• ½ lemon, zest and juice
• Toasted sesame seeds, for garnish
• Scallions, thinly sliced on an angle, for garnish
Preparation:
1. **For the chicken marinade**: Combine the chicken in a bowl with the sesame oil, sugar, soy sauce and pepper. Flip to coat, cover, refrigerate and let stand 1 hour.
2. For the pan: remove the chicken from the refrigerator. Place 1 cup of corn-starch in a shallow pot and dredge each piece of chicken, shaking off any excess.
3. Fill a high-sided saucepan or skillet with enough oil to completely submerge the chicken pieces. Heat over high heat until it shines and the temperature reaches 375 degrees F. Fry the chicken until golden brown, about 3 minutes, adding the chicken in portions to avoid overcrowding and prevent the oil from getting too hot. Place on a plate lined with paper towels.
4. In a large skillet, heat 1 tablespoon of oil over medium heat. Add the garlic and ginger and cook until golden and fragrant, about 30 seconds. Then add the rice wine, hoisin, oyster sauce, soy sauce, honey and chili sauces; bring to a boil.
5. In a glass measuring cup, mix the remaining 1 tablespoon of corn-starch with ⅛ cup very cold water (make sure the water is cold to avoid lumps!). Add the mixture to the sauce and simmer for a further minute the sauce thickens. Season as desired.
6. Add the fried chicken and toss to coat the sauce. Add the lemon zest and juice. Garnish with toasted sesame seeds and chives.

Serving Suggestion: Serve with cooked rice.
Variation Tip: Use chicken breast.
Nutritional Information Per Serving:
Calories 797 | Fat 57.5g |Sodium 1204mg | Carbs 61.5g | Fiber 1.3g | Sugar 19.2g | Protein 22.7g

Sweet & Sour Sesame Chicken Wings

Prep Time: 15 minutes plus 30 minutes for marinating.
Cook Time: 50 minutes.
Servings: 4
Ingredients:
For chicken wings:
• 1½ pounds large chicken wings
• 4 garlic cloves, minced
• 1 tablespoon fresh ginger, minced
• ¼ cup tomato sauce
• ¼ cup soy sauce
• 2 tablespoons oyster sauce
• 2 tablespoons hoisin sauce
• 2 tablespoons sambal oelek
• 2 tablespoons red wine
• 2 tablespoons fresh lemon juice
• ½ teaspoon sesame oil
• 2 tablespoons brown sugar
• ½ teaspoon five-spice powder
For topping:
• 2 tablespoons scallion, chopped
• 1 tablespoon sesame seeds
Preparation:
1. For chicken wings: in a bowl, add all the chicken wings ingredients and mix until well combined and sugar is dissolved.
2. Cover the bowl and set aside at room temperature for about 30 minutes.
3. Preheat the oven to 350 degrees F. Lightly, grease a large baking sheet.
4. Transfer the chicken wings onto the prepared baking sheet and spread in an even layer.
5. Bake for about 45-50 minutes.
6. Serve hot with the garnishing of scallion and sesame seed.
Serving Suggestions: Serve with the dipping sauce of your choice.
Variation Tip: Avoid buying the chicken wings if the flesh is too stiff.
Nutritional Information per Serving:
Calories: 408 | Fat: 14.8g|Sat Fat: 3.9g|Carbohydrates: 13.5g|Fiber: 1.3g|Sugar: 8g|Protein: 51.6g

Five-spiced Salt and Pepper Chicken

Prep Time: 15 minutes.
Cook Time: 15 minutes.
Serves: 6
Ingredients:
• 6 skinless chicken thighs, each piece chopped in half across the bone
• 2 tablespoons light soy sauce
• 1 heaping tablespoon Chinese five-spice powder
• 2 teaspoons sea salt, plus more for seasoning
• 3 cloves garlic, smashed
• 2 teaspoons toasted sesame oil
• 2 to 3 heaping tablespoons corn-starch, for dusting
• ½ cup vegetable oil, for frying
• 1 heaping tablespoon ground black pepper
• 4 to 6 sprigs fresh cilantro, chopped
Preparation:
1. Place the chicken thighs in a large bowl. Cover the chicken with the light soy sauce, Chinese five-spice powder, salt and garlic and turn to coat. Toss the chicken with the toasted sesame oil. Let marinate for as long as you have; For best results, leave the chicken in the refrigerator overnight.
2. When you're ready to roast, toss the chicken pieces in the corn-starch.
3. Heat a wok or large skillet over high heat and add vegetable oil. Working in batches so as not to clutter the pan, add the chicken and sauté lightly until the thighs are golden brown and cooked on all sides, 6 to 8 minutes. Drain the chicken on paper towels and season with salt, pepper and cilantro as soon as it comes out of the oil.
Serving Suggestion: Serve with chili garlic sauce.
Variation Tip: Use garlic powder if not getting garlic.
Nutritional Information Per Serving:
Calories 458 | Fat 30.1g |Sodium 2314mg | Carbs 8.5g | Fiber 0.3g | Sugar 3.2g | Protein 41.7g

Chinese Cashew Chicken

Prep Time: 10 minutes
Cook Time: 10 minutes
Servings: 4
Ingredients:
• 1-pound boneless, skinless chicken breasts, cubed
• 1 teaspoon sesame oil

• 2 teaspoons corn flour
• 1 egg white
• ½ teaspoon salt
• ½ teaspoon freshly ground black pepper
• 2 teaspoons groundnut oil
• ¼ cup cashews
• 1 tablespoon dry sherry
• 1 tablespoon rice wine
• 1 tablespoon light soy sauce
• ¼ cup scallion greens, chopped
Preparation:
1. In a bowl, mix together the chicken, sesame oil, corn flour, egg white, salt and pepper.
2. Set aside at room temperature for about 30 minutes.
3. In a large skillet, heat 1 teaspoon of groundnut oil over medium heat.
4. Add chicken and cook for about 3-4 minutes or until browned.
5. With a slotted spoon, transfer the chicken onto a plate.
6. In the same skillet, heat the remaining oil over medium heat and cook the cashews for about 1 minute, stirring continuously.
7. Add the sherry, wine and soy sauce and cook for 1-2 minutes until thickened.
8. Stir in the cooked chicken to the skillet and cook for about 2-3 minutes.
9. Serve immediately with the garnishing of scallion greens.
Serving Suggestions: Serve with cooked rice.
Variation Tip: Use unsalted cashews.
Nutritional Information per Serving:
Calories: 357 | Fat: 20.6g |Sat Fat: 4.5g|Carbohydrates: 6.5g|Fiber: 0.6g|Sugar: 1.7g|Protein: 35.5g

Easy Orange Chicken

Prep Time: 15 minutes
Cook Time: 4 minutes
Servings: 5
Ingredients:
• 1½ pounds boneless, skinless chicken breasts, cubed
• 1 cup chicken broth
• ½ cup fresh orange juice
• ⅓ cup distilled white vinegar
• ¼ cup soy sauce
• 2 garlic cloves, minced
• 1 tablespoon orange zest, grated
• 1 teaspoon Sriracha
• ½ cup sugar
• ¼ teaspoon ground ginger
• ¼ teaspoon salt
• ¼ teaspoon ground white pepper
• 2 large eggs, beaten

- 1 cup corn flour
- 1 cup vegetable oil
- 2 tablespoons scallion greens, sliced
- ½ teaspoon sesame seeds

Preparation:
1. In a bowl, add the chicken, broth, orange juice, vinegar, soy sauce, garlic, orange zest, Sriracha, sugar, ground ginger, salt and white pepper and mix well.
2. Cover the bowl and refrigerate to marinade for 30 minutes.
3. Remove the chicken from bowl and reserve the marinate.
4. In a shallow bowl, place the eggs.
5. In another shallow bowl, place the corn flour.
6. Dip the chicken cubes into the beaten egg and then coat with corn flour.
7. In a large skillet, heat oil over medium heat and cook the chicken cubes for about 2-4 minutes or until golden brown.
8. With a slotted spoon, transfer the chicken cubes onto a paper towel-line plate to drain.
9. Now transfer the chicken cubes onto a serving platter and top with reserved marinade.
10. Garnish with scallion greens and sesame seeds and serve.

Serving Suggestions: Serve alongside the orange slices.

Variation Tip: For the best result, use freshly squeezed orange juice.

Nutritional Information per Serving:
Calories: 867 | Fat: 57.1g|Sat Fat: 12.2g|Carbohydrates: 43.1g|Fiber: 2.1g|Sugar: 22.8g|Protein: 45.6g

Chinese Roasted Goose

Prep Time: 15 minutes
Cook Time: 4 hours
Servings: 12
Ingredients:
- 10 pounds goose, neck and giblets removed
- Salt and freshly ground black pepper, to taste
- 2 tablespoons Chinese black vinegar
- 2 medium apples, cored and chopped
- 5 bulbs garlic, unpeeled
- 2 cups Shaoxing wine

Preparation:
1. Preheat the oven to 325 degrees F. Arrange a wire rack in a roasting pan.

2. With a fork, prick the skin of goose at many places.
3. Season inside and outside of goose with the salt and black pepper evenly.
4. Now rub the skin of goose with ¼ of the black vinegar.
5. Stuff the cavity of goose with the apples and garlic bulbs.
6. Arrange the goose into the prepared roasting pan, breast side up.
7. Add a small amount of water in the roasting pan.
8. With a large piece of foil, cover the roasting pan and roast for about 3 hours.
9. Remove the roasting pan from oven and then carefully uncover the goose.
10. With a fork, prick the skin of goose again.
11. Carefully pour the wine over the goose and roast, uncovered for about 1 hour.
12. Remove from the oven and palace the goose onto a platter for about 10-15 minutes before carving.
13. With a sharp knife, cut the goose into desired sized pieces and serve.

Serving Suggestions: Serve with your roasted veggies.

Variation Tip: If you are using a frozen goose, then thaw it completely before seasoning.

Nutritional Information per Serving:
Calories: 969| Fat: 48g|Sat Fat: 17.3g|Carbohydrates: 10g|Fiber: 1.1g|Sugar: 4.3g|Protein: 110g

Mango & Pepper Chicken with Shallot

Prep Time: 15 minutes plus 30 minutes for marinating.
Cook Time: 7 minutes.
Servings: 4
Ingredients:
For chicken marinade:
- ¾ pound boneless, skinless chicken breast, sliced
- 1½ teaspoons soy sauce
- 1 teaspoon corn-starch
- ¼ teaspoon salt
- Pinch of ground white pepper

For sauce:
- 2 teaspoons cider vinegar
- 1½ teaspoons ketchup
- 1½ teaspoons sugar
- 2 tablespoons water

For cooking:
- 1 tablespoon canola oil
- 1 Star anise, crushed lightly
- ½ medium red bell pepper, seeded and sliced
- ½ medium green bell pepper, seeded and sliced

- 1 large shallot, chopped
- 1 tablespoon fresh ginger, grated
- 1 teaspoon garlic, minced
- 2 large mangoes, peeled, pitted and sliced thinly

Preparation:
For marinade:
1. In a bowl, add all ingredients and mix well.
2. Cover the bowl and refrigerate to marinade for about 30 minutes.

For sauce:
3. In a bowl, add all ingredients and beat until well combined. Set aside.
4. In a non-stick skillet, heat oil with star anise over high heat and stir fry the chicken slices for about 3 minutes.
5. Add bell peppers, shallot, ginger, and garlic and stir fry for about 1-2 minutes.
6. Stir in the sauce and stir fry for about 1 minute.
7. Stir in the mango slices and stir fry for about 1 minute.
8. Serve hot.

Serving Suggestions: Serve with the garnishing of sesame seeds.
Variation Tip: Use ripe mango.
Nutritional Information per Serving:
Calories: 279 | Fat: 6.5g|Sat Fat: 0.4g|Carbohydrates: 37.4g|Fiber: 3.3g|Sugar: 31.6g|Protein: 20.2g

Honey-glazed Roasted Duck

Prep Time: 15 minutes
Cook Time: 1 hour 35 minutes
Servings: 6
Ingredients:
- 1 (4-pound) whole duck, giblets removed
- ½ teaspoon ground cinnamon
- ½ teaspoon ground ginger
- ¼ teaspoon ground nutmeg
- ⅛ teaspoon ground cloves
- ¼ teaspoon ground white pepper
- 3 tablespoons soy sauce, divided
- 1 scallion, halved
- 1 tablespoon honey
- 1 orange, cut into rounds

Preparation:
1. In a small bowl, mix together the spices and white pepper.
2. Rub the cavity of duck with 1 teaspoon of spice mixture.
3. In the remaining spice mixture, add 1 tablespoon of soy sauce and mix well.
4. Rub the outside of duck with soy sauce mixture generously.
5. Stuff the cavity with scallion.

6. With a large piece of foil, cover the duck and refrigerate for at least 2 hours.
7. In a large pan of water, arrange a rack over medium-high heat.
8. Arrange the duck over rack, breast side up and steam, covered for about 1 hour. (You can add more water in the pan, if necessary).
9. Carefully remove the duck from pan and place in a large colander to drain.
10. Remove the scallion from cavity and discard it.
11. Preheat the oven to 375 degrees F.
12. With a fork, prick the skin of duck.
13. Arrange the duck into a roasting pan, breast side up.
14. Roast for about 30 minutes.
15. Meanwhile, in a small bowl, add the remaining soy sauce and honey and mix well.
16. After 30 minutes of roasting, remove the roasting pan from oven and coat the duck with honey mixture evenly.
17. Place the roasting pan in oven and immediately set the temperature to 500 degrees F.
18. Roast for about 5 minutes or until the skin is richly browned.
19. Remove from the oven and palace the duck onto a platter for about 10-15 minutes before carving.
20. With a sharp knife, cut the duck into desired sized pieces and serve.

Serving Suggestions: Serve with the garnishing of orange slices.
Variation Tip: Make sure to pat dry the duck completely before seasoning.
Nutritional Information per Serving:
Calories: 640 | Fat: 34g|Sat Fat: 12.6g|Carbohydrates: 7.7g|Fiber: 1.1g|Sugar: 6g|Protein: 71.9g

Aromatic Duck Breast

Prep Time: 15 minutes
Cook Time: 34 minutes
Servings: 6
Ingredients:
- ¼ cup Shaoxing wine
- ¼ cup hoisin sauce
- ½ teaspoon five-spice powder
- 4 garlic cloves, peeled
- 1 (1-inch) piece fresh ginger, peeled
- 4 (12-ounce) duck breasts
- ½ teaspoon salt

Preparation:
1. In a small food processor, add the wine, hoisin sauce, five-spice powder, garlic and ginger and pulse until smooth.
2. Transfer the paste into a baking dish.
3. Season the duck breasts with slat evenly.
4. Add the duck breasts into the baking dish and coat with paste generously.

5. Set aside at room temperature for about 30-60 minutes.
6. Preheat the oven to 425 degrees F.
7. Remove the duck breasts from baking dish and with paper towels pat dry them.
8. With a knife, score the skin about ½-inch apart in a diamond pattern.
9. In a cold 12-inch heavy-bottomed ovenproof skillet, place duck breasts, skin-side down.
10. Place the skillet over medium heat and cook for about 1-2 minutes.
11. Reduce the heat to medium-low heat and sear for about 10-12 minutes.
12. Flip the duck breasts and sear for about 3-4 minutes.
13. Now arrange the duck breasts in the skillet, skin-side down.
14. Transfer the skillet into the oven and bake for about 8 minutes.
15. Flip the duck breasts and bake for about 6-8 minutes.
16. Remove from the oven and palace the duck breasts onto a platter for about 10 minutes before carving.
17. Cut each duck breast into desired sized slices and serve.

Serving Suggestions: Serve with plum sauce.
Variation Tip: Dry sherry can be used instead of wine.
Nutritional Information per Serving:
Calories: 328 | Fat: 9.5g|Sat Fat: 0.1g|Carbohydrates: 5.8g|Fiber: 0.4g|Sugar: 3g|Protein: 50.4g

Sweet General Tso's Chicken

Prep Time: 20 minutes.
Cook Time: 10 minutes.

Serves:2
Ingredients:
• ½ pound boneless, skinless chicken breast, cut into 1-inch pieces
• Sea salt and freshly ground white pepper
• ½ tablespoon corn-starch
Sweet Sauce:
• ¼ cup chicken stock
• ½ tablespoon Guilin chili sauce or Sriracha
• ½ tablespoon ketchup
• ½ tablespoon light soy sauce
• ½ tablespoon rice vinegar
• ½ tablespoon yellow bean sauce (soy bean paste)
• ½ teaspoon honey
• ¼ teaspoon dark soy sauce
Stir-Fry:
• ½ tablespoon vegetable oil
• 1 clove garlic, peeled, left whole and crushed
• ½ tablespoon Shao sing rice wine or dry sherry
• 2 whole dried Sichuan chilies
• 1 scallion, chopped
• ½ cup peanuts, toasted and chopped
• 4 ounces' egg noodles, cooked per package instructions
Preparation:
1. **For the chicken:** In a large bowl, sprinkle the chicken with a pinch of salt and pepper. Add the corn-starch and mix well.
2. **For the sweet sauce**: In another bowl, add the broth, chili sauce, tomato sauce, light soy sauce, rice vinegar, yellow bean sauce, honey and dark soy sauce and set aside.
3. **For the stir fry**: heat a wok over high heat and when the wok begins to smoke, and then add the vegetable oil. Add the garlic and chicken pieces and let the chicken rest in the wok for 1 minute before frying for another 2 minutes. When the chicken begins to turn opaque, add the rice wine and the dried peppers and cook for a few seconds. Then add the sweet sauce mixture and cook for another 3 minutes. Cook chicken in sauce until cooked through and sauce is reduced, slightly sticky and thicker, 1 to 2 minutes more. Add the scallions and peanuts and cook for less than 1 minute. Add the noodles and transfer them to a serving plate.
Serving Suggestion: Serve with salad.
Variation Tip: Use any kind of noodles.
Nutritional Information Per Serving:
Calories 500 | Fat 25.5g |Sodium 2104mg | Carbs 33.5g | Fiber 2g | Sugar 6.2g | Protein 32.7g

Spicy Pork with Tofu

Prep Time: 15 minutes
Cook Time: 25 minutes
Servings: 2
Ingredients:
For marinade:
• 4 ounces ground pork
• 2 teaspoons Shaoxing wine
• 1 teaspoon light soy sauce
• ½ teaspoon fresh ginger, minced
For braising:
• 1 teaspoon corn-starch
• 1 tablespoon water
• 1 tablespoon vegetable oil
• 2 teaspoons Sichuan peppercorns
• 3 tablespoons spicy bean sauce
• 2 tablespoons scallion, chopped
• 1 (14-ounce) block firm tofu, pressed, drained and cut into ½-inch cubes
• 1 cup chicken broth
• 2 teaspoons chili oil
• 1 teaspoon sugar
• ¼ teaspoon five-spice powder
• 1 tablespoon scallion greens, chopped
Preparation:
1. For marinade: in a bowl, add all ingredients and mix well.
2. For braising: in a small bowl, dissolve corn-starch in water. Set aside.
3. In a large non-stick skillet, heat the vegetable oil over medium-high heat. And sauté the peppercorns for about 40-60 seconds or until dark brown.
4. With a spatula, remove the peppercorns.
5. In the same skillet with oil, add the pork mixture and bean sauce over medium heat and stir fry for about 3-4 minutes.
6. Add scallion and stir fry for about 1 minute.
7. Stir in the tofu, broth, chili oil, sugar and five-spice powder and bring to a gentle simmer.
8. Reduce the heat to low and simmer, covered for about 10-15 minutes.
9. Add in the corn-starch mixture and cook for about 1-2 minutes, stirring continuously.
10. Serve hot with the garnishing of scallion greens.
Serving Suggestions: Serve with boiled rice.
Variation Tip: If the dish is too spicy, add another teaspoon of sugar.
Nutritional Information per Serving:
Calories: 406 | Fat: 24.7g|Sat Fat: 4.6g|Carbohydrates: 14.1g|Fiber: 2g|Sugar: 8.3g|Protein: 35.3g

Savory Fried Pork Liver

Prep Time: 15 minutes
Cook Time: 6 minutes
Servings: 2
Ingredients:
• ½ teaspoon fresh ginger, grated
• ¼ teaspoon garlic, minced
• 3 tablespoons soy sauce
• 1 tablespoon fish sauce
• 1 tablespoon fresh lemon juice
• 1 teaspoon erythritol
• Freshly ground black pepper, to taste
• 10½ ounces pork liver, cut into ¼-inch slices
• 2 tablespoons olive oil
• 10 scallions, cut into two-inch lengths
Preparation:
1. In a bowl, add the ginger, garlic, soy sauce, fish sauce, lemon juice, Erythritol and black pepper and mix well.
2. Add the liver slices and coat with the mixture generously.
3. Cover the bowl and refrigerate to marinate for at least 2 hours.
4. Remove the liver slices from bowl, reserving the marinade.
5. In a large skillet, heat the oil and cook liver slices for about 2 minutes, without stirring.
6. Flip and cook for about 1 minute.
7. Add half of the scallions and reserved marinade and stir fry for about 1-2 minutes.
8. Stir in the remaining scallions and remove from the heat.
9. Serve hot.
Serving Suggestions: Serve with favorite steamed veggies.
Variation Tip: For better taste, try to consume the pork liver within 1-2 days after purchase.
Nutritional Information per Serving:
Calories: 417 | Fat: 20.8g|Sat Fat: 4.2g|Carbohydrates: 15.9g|Fiber: 2.3g|Sugar: 4.7g|Protein: 42.2g

Pork and Cabbage Dumplings

Prep Time: 10 minutes.
Cook Time: 15 to 20 minutes.
Serves: 6
Ingredients:
• 1 ¾ pounds ground pork
• 1 tablespoon minced fresh ginger root
• 4 cloves garlic, minced
• 2 tablespoons thinly sliced green onion
• 4 tablespoons soy sauce
• 3 tablespoons sesame oil
• 1 egg, beaten
• 5 cups finely shredded Chinese cabbage
Preparation:
1. In a large bowl, combine the pork, ginger, garlic, spring onions, soy sauce, sesame oil, egg and cabbage. Stir until everything is well combined.
2. Place 1 heaping teaspoon of pork filling on each wonton skin. Wet the edges with water and fold the edges into a triangle. Roll edges lightly to seal filling. Set the meatballs aside on a lightly floured surface until cooked through.
3. Cook the meatballs in a covered bamboo or metal steamer for about 15 to 20 minutes. Use immediately.
Serving Suggestion: Serve with chili garlic sauce.
Variation Tip: Use coconut amions.
Nutritional Information Per Serving:
Calories 126 | Fat 10.3g |Sodium 664mg | Carbs 2.7g | Fiber 0.8g | Sugar 1g | Protein 6g

Pork and Ginger Stir-Fry

Prep Time: 15 minutes.
Cook Time: 15 minutes.
Serves: 4
Ingredients:
• 1-inch piece fresh ginger root, thinly sliced
• ½ pound thinly sliced lean pork
• 2 teaspoons soy sauce

• 1 teaspoon dark soy sauce
• 1 teaspoon salt
• ¼ teaspoon sugar
• 4 teaspoons sesame oil
• 2 green onions, chopped
• 2 tablespoons Chinese rice wine
Preparation:
1. Heat the oil in a large skillet or wok over medium heat. Fry the ginger in hot oil until fragrant, then add the pork, soy sauce, dark soy sauce, salt and sugar. Cook for 10 minutes, stirring occasionally.
2. Add sesame oil, spring onion and rice wine. Cook over low heat until the pork is tender.
Serving Suggestion: Serve with rice.
Variation Tip: Use honey if you want healthy version.
Nutritional Information Per Serving:
Calories 174 | Fat 7.9g |Sodium 2560mg | Carbs 7.9g | Fiber 0.2g | Sugar 7g | Protein 16.8g

Chinese Flavored Pork Tenderloin

Prep Time: 05 minutes.
Cook Time: 35 minutes.
Serves: 6
Ingredients:
• 2 (1 ½ pound) pork tenderloins, trimmed
• 2 tablespoons light soy sauce
• 2 tablespoons hoisin sauce
• 1 tablespoon sherry
• 1 tablespoon black bean sauce
• 1½ teaspoons minced fresh ginger root
• 1½ teaspoons packed brown sugar
• 1 clove garlic
• ½ teaspoon sesame oil
• 1 pinch Chinese five-spice powder
Preparation:
1. Place the beef tenderloins in a flat glass bowl. In a small bowl, combine soy sauce, hoisin sauce, sherry, black bean sauce, ginger, sugar, garlic, sesame oil and five-spice powder. Pour the marinade over the pork and turn to coat. Cover and refrigerate for at least 2 hours or up to 24 hours.
2. Preheat the oven to 375 degrees F (190 degrees C). Take the roast beef out of the refrigerator while the oven is preheating.
3. Bake the pork in the preheated oven for 30 to 35 minutes, or until done. Let stand 10 minutes then cut diagonally into thin slices.
Serving Suggestion: Serve with chili garlic sauce.
Variation Tip: Use Tempeh if you want vegan version.
Nutritional Information Per Serving:
Calories 493 | Fat 19.1g |Sodium 1835mg | Carbs 9.3g | Fiber 0.2g | Sugar 5.8g | Protein 69.7g

Stir-fried Pork and Bamboo Shoots

Prep Time: 15 minutes.
Cook Time: 15 minutes.
Serves:4
Ingredients:
- 3 tablespoons peanut oil
- 1 (14-ounce) can thinly sliced bamboo shoots
- 2 cloves garlic, minced
- 1 fresh red chili pepper, seeded and minced
- ½ teaspoon crushed red pepper flakes
- 3 ounces ground pork
- 1 teaspoon Shaoxing rice wine
- salt to taste
- 2 teaspoons rice vinegar
- 2 teaspoons soy sauce
- 3 tablespoons chicken broth
- 3 green onions, thinly sliced
- 1 teaspoon sesame oil

Preparation:
1. Heat a tablespoon of peanut oil in a wok over medium heat. Put bamboo shoots in the pan; fry until dry and fragrant, about 3 minutes. Take out of the wok and keep.
2. Turn the heat up to high and pour in the remaining peanut oil. Quickly fry the garlic, red chilli and red pepper flakes in the hot oil until they are fragrant. Add the pork and keep frying until cooked through. Pour the rice wine; Season to taste with salt.
3. Return the bamboo shoots to the wok and heat until they sizzle. Add rice vinegar, soy sauce, chicken broth, and extra salt to taste. Cook for 1 to 2 minutes and stir to allow the aroma to penetrate the bamboo shoots. At the end of the cooking process, add the green onions. Take the wok off the stove; add the sesame oil before serving.
Serving Suggestion: Serve with rice.
Variation Tip: Use pork broth.
Nutritional Information Per Serving:
Calories 108 | Fat 5.7g |Sodium 242mg | Carbs 6.7g | Fiber 2.3g | Sugar 3.2g | Protein 8.7g

Pork Lo Mein with Snap Peas

Prep Time: 15 minutes.
Cook Time: 15 minutes.
Serves:4
Ingredients:
- 1 (8 ounce) package linguine
- ⅓ cup low-sodium soy sauce
- 2 tablespoons rice vinegar
- 2 teaspoons corn-starch
- 1 teaspoon white sugar
- ½ teaspoon sesame oil
- 2 tablespoons rapeseed oil
- 2 cups snap peas
- 1 small sweet onion, chopped
- 1 (12-ounce) pork tenderloin, cut into thin strips
- 1 (8-ounce) package sliced white mushrooms
- 1 red bell pepper, chopped
- 1 clove garlic, chopped
- ½ teaspoon chopped fresh ginger, or to taste
- 2 cloves garlic, chopped
- 3 green onions, sliced

Preparation:
1. Bring a large pot of lightly salted water to a boil; Simmer linguine until al dente, 8 to 9 minutes; flow out.
2. In a small bowl, combine the soy sauce, vinegar, corn-starch, sugar and sesame oil.
3. Heat rapeseed oil in a large skillet over medium heat; Boil and stir the peas and onions in the hot oil until the onion is tender, about 2 minutes. Add the pork, mushrooms, red pepper, 1 garlic clove and ginger; cook until pork is no longer pink, about 2 minutes.
4. Mix 2 garlic cloves with the pork mixture; Cook for 1 minute. Pour soy sauce mixture over pork mixture; cook and stir until sauce thickens, about 1 minute. Remove the pan from the fire. Add linguine to mixture; toss to coat. Sprinkle with spring onions.
Serving Suggestion: Serve with chili garlic sauce.
Variation Tip: Use any kind of noodles.
Nutritional Information Per Serving:
Calories 464 | Fat 12.4g |Sodium 1260mg | Carbs 51.7g | Fiber 5.3g | Sugar 9.2g | Protein 36.7g

Scrumptious Barbeque Pork

Prep Time: 10 minutes plus 4 to 12 hours for marinating.
Cook Time: 2 hours.
Serves:6
Ingredients:
- ⅔ cup soy sauce
- ½ cup honey
- ½ cup Chinese rice wine
- ⅓ cup hoisin sauce
- ⅓ cup ketchup
- ⅓ cup brown sugar
- 4 cloves garlic, crushed
- 1 teaspoon Chinese five-spice powder
- ½ teaspoon freshly ground black pepper

- ¼ teaspoon cayenne pepper
- ⅛ teaspoon pink curing salt
- 1 (3-pound) boneless pork butt (shoulder)
- 1 teaspoon red food colouring, or as desired (Optional)
- 1 teaspoon kosher salt, or to taste

Preparation:
1. Put the soy sauce, honey, rice wine, hoisin sauce, tomato sauce, brown sugar, garlic, five-spice powder, black pepper, cayenne pepper and curing salt in a saucepan. Bring to a boil over high heat; Reduce the heat to medium-high. Cook for 1 minute. Remove the stove. Let cool to room temperature.
2. Cut roast pork in half lengthwise. Cut each half lengthwise into 4 long, thick pieces of pork.
3. Place the cooled sauce in a large mixing bowl. Add the red food colouring. Put the pieces of pork in the sauce and garnish each piece. Cover with plastic wrap and refrigerate for 4 to 12 hours.
4. Preheat the grill to medium heat, 275 to 300 degrees F (135 to 150 degrees C) and lightly grease the grill. Line a baking sheet with parchment paper.
5. Remove the pieces of pork from the marinade and drain off the excess. Place on a prepared baking sheet. Sprinkle with kosher salt to taste.
6. Transfer the grilled cuts of pork over indirect heat to the prepared grill. Cover and cook for about 45 minutes. Brush with marinade; Tower. Continue cooking until an instant thermometer reads 185 to 190 degrees F in the middle, about 1 hour and 15 minutes more. Do not use marinade on cooked meat until after cooking.
7. Place the remaining marinade in a saucepan; bring to a boil; Simmer for 1 minute. Remove the stove. You can now use it to spread over cooked pork.

Serving Suggestion: Serve with noodles.
Variation Tip: Use dry sherry if not available Chinese rice wine.
Nutritional Information Per Serving:
Calories 622 | Fat 15.7g |Sodium 2110mg | Carbs 43.8g | Fiber 0.8g | Sugar 38.2g | Protein 73.1g

Classic Peking Pork Chops

Prep Time: 15 minutes.
Cook Time: 4 to 6 hours.
Serves:6
Ingredients:
- 6 thick cut pork chops (1 inch)
- ¼ cup brown sugar
- 1 teaspoon ground ginger
- ½ cup soy sauce
- ¼ cup ketchup
- 1 clove garlic, crushed
- salt and pepper to taste

Preparation:
1. Remove excess fat from the pork chops and place them in the slow cooker. Combine brown sugar, ginger, soy sauce, tomato sauce, garlic, salt and pepper in a small bowl and pour over meat.
2. Cover, reduce heat to a simmer and cook 4 to 6 hours or until just tender. Season with salt and pepper if necessary.
Serving Suggestion: Serve with chili garlic sauce.
Variation Tip: Use honey if you want healthy version.
Nutritional Information Per Serving:
Calories 176 | Fat 3.1g |Sodium 1540mg | Carbs 11.5g | Fiber 0.3g | Sugar 9.2g | Protein 23.7g

Sweet & Sour Pork Tenderloin

Prep Time: 15 minutes
Cook Time: 15 minutes
Servings: 4
Ingredients:
For sauce:
- ¼ cup apple cider vinegar
- ½ cup soy sauce
- 3 tablespoons honey
- 1 tablespoon corn-starch
- 4 garlic cloves, minced
- 1½ tablespoons fresh ginger, minced

For pork mixture:
- 2 tablespoons coconut oil
- 1 pound pork tenderloin, cut into bite-sized pieces
- 1 medium pineapple, peeled, cored and cut into bite-sized chunks
- 3 bell peppers (green and red), seeded and cubed
- 1 red onion, chopped
- 2 scallions, sliced

Preparation:
1. For sauce: in a bowl, add all ingredients and beat until well combined. Set aside.
2. In a large skillet, melt the coconut oil over medium-high heat and cook the pork pieces for about 8 minutes.
3. Add the pineapple, bell peppers and onion and stir to combine.
4. Increase the heat to high and cook for about 2-3 minutes, stirring frequently.
5. Stir in the sauce and cook for about 2-3 minutes or until desired thickness of sauce.
6. Remove from the heat and immediately stir in the scallions.
Serving Suggestions: Serve with hot steamed rice.
Variation Tip: Make sure to use fresh pineapple.
Nutritional Information per Serving:
Calories: 449 | Fat: 11.4g|Sat Fat: 7.3g|Carbohydrates: 55.9g|Fiber: 5.4g|Sugar: 39.2g|Protein: 34.5g

Braised Pork Spare Ribs

Prep Time: 05 minutes.
Cook Time: 1 hour 15 minutes.
Serves:4
Ingredients:
- 1 pound pork spareribs, cut into 3 inch pieces
- 1 tablespoon vegetable oil
- 1 (1-inch) piece fresh ginger root, sliced
- 5 green onions cut into 2-inch pieces
- ½ teaspoon ground cinnamon
- 2 cups water
- 1 ½ tablespoons soy sauce
- 1 teaspoon white sugar
- 1 teaspoon rice wine
- ¼ teaspoon salt
- ¼ teaspoon pepper

Preparation:
1. Bring a large pot of water to a boil, then add the ribs and cook, uncovered, for 3 to 5 minutes. Drain in a colander and keep.
2. Heat the vegetable oil in a pan over high heat. Add ginger, spring onions and cinnamon; cook and stir until fragrant. Add the ribs and cook for 3 to 5 minutes. Pour in the water, soy sauce, sugar and rice wine.
3. Season with salt and pepper. Bring the mixture to a boil, then lower the heat to low and cover. Cook over low heat until ribs are tender, about 1 hour.
Serving Suggestion: Serve with rice.
Variation Tip: Use normal bread crumbs.
Nutritional Information Per Serving:
Calories 356 | Fat 30.7g |Sodium 481mg | Carbs 2.7g | Fiber 0.7g | Sugar 1.2g | Protein 18.7g

Authentic Chinese Pearl Meatballs

Prep Time: 15 minutes.
Cook Time: 30 minutes.
Serves:4
Ingredients:
- ½ cup uncooked glutinous (sticky) white rice, rinsed
- ⅔ pound ground pork
- 2 tablespoons water

- 1 tablespoon Chinese cooking wine
- 1 tablespoon corn-starch
- 1 tablespoon soy sauce
- 1 small onion, chopped
- ½ teaspoon grated fresh ginger
- ½ teaspoon minced garlic
- ½ teaspoon salt
- 1 dash ground black pepper
- 2 leaves Chinese cabbage

Preparation:
1. Put the rice in a bowl with enough water to cover it. Leave to soak for 2 hours. Drain and place in a bowl.
2. Combine ground pork, water, wine, corn starch, soy sauce, onion, ginger, garlic, salt and pepper in a bowl until all ingredients are well combined. mixed. Divide and roll the mixture into 1½- to 2-inch balls. Roll the meatballs in the soaked sticky rice until completely coated.
3. Line a large bamboo steamer with the cabbage leaves. Place the meatballs on the cabbage leaves.
4. Bring a large pot of water to a boil over high heat; Place a bamboo steamer over the boiling water. Steam the meatballs for about 30 minutes until they are no longer pink in the middle
Serving Suggestion: Serve with chili garlic sauce.
Variation Tip: Use normal bread crumbs.
Nutritional Information Per Serving:
Calories 158 | Fat 1.7g |Sodium 567mg | Carbs 10.7g | Fiber 0.6g | Sugar 0.2g | Protein 20.7g

Chinese Pork Belly (Dong Po)

Prep Time: 15 minutes.
Cook Time: 2 hours 40 minutes.
Serves:6
Ingredients:
- 1-pound raw pork belly
- 3 tablespoons vegetable oil
- ¼ cup light soy sauce
- ¼ cup dark soy sauce
- ½ cup Chinese rice cooking wine
- 3 ½ ounces Chinese rock sugar
- 1 (1-inch) piece fresh ginger, peeled and grated
- 8 spring onions, sliced

Preparation:
1. Cut the pork belly into 2-cm-wide strips. Bring a large pot of water to a boil and add the pork slices; Lower the heat and simmer the meat for 10 minutes. Remove from the water and dry with absorbent paper.
2. Heat the vegetable oil in a large wok over medium heat and brown the pork strips well on all sides. The pork will splash - use splash guard for this step.
3. While the pork is browning, combine the light soy sauce, dark soy sauce, rice wine, rock sugar, ginger and chives in a large saucepan or pot. Bring the mixture to a boil and stir to dissolve the sugar.

4. Lower the heat and simmer the pork strips in the liquid. Cover and simmer until meat is very tender, 1 ½ to 2 hours. Add water as needed to prevent the liquid from drying out completely.
Serving Suggestion: Serve with salad.
Variation Tip: Use white granulated sugar if not access Chinese rock sugar.
Nutritional Information Per Serving:
Calories 425 | Fat 27.2g |Sodium 1560mg | Carbs 2.7g | Fiber 0.5g | Sugar 1.9g | Protein 34.4g

Sweet & Sour Glazed Pork Chops

Prep Time: 15 minutes
Cook Time: 18 minutes
Servings: 4
Ingredients:
- ½ cup rice vinegar
- 3 tablespoons mirin
- 3 tablespoons fresh orange juice
- ⅓ cup brown sugar
- 1 teaspoon fresh ginger, grated
- Pinch of red pepper flakes, crushed
- 4 (6-ounce) boneless pork loin chops
- 1 tablespoon vegetable oil
- 1 scallion, chopped
- 1 teaspoon sesame seeds, toasted

Preparation:
1. For glaze: in a small bowl, add the vinegar, mirin, orange juice, brown sugar and ginger and beat until sugar dissolves completely. Set aside.
2. With a knife, make ½-inch deep cuts on the silver skin edge of the pork chops about 1-inch apart.
3. With paper towels, pat dry the chops completely and then season with salt and black pepper evenly.
4. In a large skillet, heat the vegetable oil over medium-high heat and cook the pork chops for about 4 minutes.
5. Flip the chops and cook for about 1-2 minutes.
6. Transfer the hops onto a plate and cover with a piece of foil for about 5 minutes.
7. In the same skillet, add the glaze over medium heat and cook for about 2-5 minutes, stirring continuously.
8. Return the cooked pork chops into the skillet and cook for about 1-2 minutes, coating with glaze evenly.
9. Transfer the chops onto a platter and top with any remaining glaze.
10. Garnish with scallion and sesame seeds and serve immediately.
Serving Suggestions: Serve with fresh salad.

Variation Tip: Choose pork chops with a pinkish color.
Nutritional Information per Serving:
Calories: 370 | Fat: 9.8g |Sat Fat: 2.8g|Carbohydrates: 19.1g|Fiber: 0.3g|Sugar: 15.8g|Protein: 44.9g

Sticky Sweet Pork

Prep Time: 10 minutes
Cook Time: 12 minutes
Servings: 6
Ingredients:
- ½ cup mild honey
- 2-4 tablespoons sriracha
- 1 tablespoon rice wine vinegar
- 1½ pounds boneless center cut pork loin, cut into ¼-inch thick strips
- Salt and freshly ground black pepper, to taste
- 1 tablespoon peanut oil
- 1 (2-inch) piece fresh ginger, grated
- 5 garlic cloves, minced
- 1 tablespoon sesame seeds

Preparation:
1. In a small bowl, add the honey, sriracha and vinegar and mix well. Set aside.
2. Season the pork strips with salt and black pepper.
3. In a heavy-bottomed skillet, heat the oil over medium-high heat and sear the pork strips for about 4-5 minutes or until browned completely.
4. With a slotted spoon, transfer the pork strips onto a plate.
5. In the same skillet, add the ginger and garlic and sauté for about 30 seconds.
6. Add the honey mixture and stir to combine.
7. Increase the heat to high and bring to a boil, stirring frequently.
8. Stir in the cooked pork strips and cook for about 2-3 minutes or until desired thickness of sauce.
9. Serve hot with the garnishing of sesame seeds.
Serving Suggestions: Serve over cooked noodles.
Variation Tip: You can use chili garlic sauce instead of sriracha.
Nutritional Information per Serving:
Calories: 290 | Fat: 7g|Sat Fat: 12.8g|Carbohydrates: 26.1g|Fiber: 0.4g|Sugar: 22.3g|Protein: 30.2g

Pork and Bok Choy

Prep Time: 15 minutes
Cook Time: 13 minutes
Servings: 4
Ingredients:
• 1 tablespoon extra-virgin olive oil
• 4 scallions, chopped
• 2 garlic cloves, minced
• 2 tablespoons fresh ginger, minced
• 1 Serrano pepper, chopped finely
• 1 pound pork loin steaks, trimmed and cut into strips
• 1 pound Bok choy, sliced
• 4 tablespoons low-sodium soy sauce
Preparation:
1. In a large skillet, heat oil over medium heat and sauté the scallion for about 2 minutes.
2. Add the garlic, ginger, scallions and Serrano pepper and sauté for about 1 minute.
3. Add pork and cook for about 4-5 minutes.
4. Add Bok choy and soy sauce and cook for about 4-5 minutes.
5. Serve hot.
Serving Suggestions: Serve with cooked jasmine rice.
Variation Tip: Make sure to pick pork that is reddish-pink and firm.
Nutritional Information per Serving:
Calories: 341 | Fat: 19.7g|Sat Fat: 6.5g|Carbohydrates: 7.1g|Fiber: 2g|Sugar: 2.9g|Protein: 34.3g

Chinese Braised Pork Belly

Prep Time: 15 minutes
Cook Time: 2 hours 10 minutes
Servings: 6
Ingredients:
• 1 pound pork belly, cut into 2-inch-wide strips

• 3 tablespoons vegetable oil
• ½ cup Chinese rice cooking wine
• ¼ cup dark soy sauce
• ¼ cup light soy sauce
• 3½ ounces Chinese rock sugar
• 8 scallions, sliced
• 1 (1-inch) piece fresh ginger, peeled and grated
Preparation:
1. In a large pan of boiling water, add the pork strips and cook for about 10 minutes.
2. Drain the pork strips and with paper towels, pat dry them.
3. In a large skillet, heat the oil over medium-high heat and sear the pork strips for about 4-5 minutes or until browned completely.
4. Meanwhile, in a large pan, add the remaining ingredients and bring to a boil, stirring continuously.
5. Add the pork strips and stir to combine.
6. Reduce the heat to low and simmer, covered for about 1½-2 hours.
7. Serve hot.
Serving Suggestions: Serve alongside the steamed greens of your choice.
Variation Tip: While simmering, you can add the water to avoid dryness.
Nutritional Information per Serving:
Calories: 527 | Fat: 27.3g|Sat Fat: 10.1g|Carbohydrates: 29.6g|Fiber: 0.8g|Sugar: 22.7g|Protein: 36.7g

Stir-fried Pork & Asparagus

Prep Time: 15 minutes
Cook Time: 10 minutes
Servings: 4
Ingredients:
• ⅓ cup low-sodium soy sauce, divided
• 2 tablespoons Shaoxing rice wine
• 4 teaspoons corn-starch
• 1¼ pounds ground pork
• 2 tablespoons sesame oil, divided
• 1 bunch asparagus spears, trimmed and cut into 1-inch pieces
• 2 tablespoons fresh ginger, minced
• 1 tablespoon chili garlic sauce
• ½ cup oyster sauce
• 1½ tablespoons honey
• 3 scallions, chopped
Preparation:
1. In a bowl, add 2 tablespoons of soy sauce, wine and corn-starch and beat until corn-starch dissolves completely.
2. Add pork and gently stir to combine.
3. In a large non-stick skillet, heat 1 tablespoon of sesame oil over high heat and cook the asparagus, ginger and chili sauce for about 3 minutes, stirring frequently.

4. With a slotted spoon, transfer the asparagus mixture onto a plate and set aside.
5. In the same skillet, heat the remaining sesame oil over medium-high heat and stir fry the pork mixture for about 4 minutes or until browned, crumbling the meat frequently.
6. Stir in the cooked asparagus, remaining soy sauce, oyster sauce, scallions, and honey and stir fry for about 2 minutes.
Serving Suggestions: Serve alongside the fresh green salad.
Variation Tip: Choose fresh green beans for this dish.
Nutritional Information per Serving:
Calories: 356 | Fat: 12.1g|Sat Fat: 2.8g|Carbohydrates: 21.8g|Fiber: 3.1g|Sugar: 12.3g|Protein: 41.5g

Glazed Marinated Pork Ribs

Prep Time: 15 minutes plus 4 hours for marinating.
Cook Time: 55 minutes.
Servings: 2
Ingredients:
• 5 garlic cloves, minced
• 1 tablespoon sweet pineapple, minced
• 5 tablespoons ketchup
• 2 tablespoons honey
• 2 tablespoons tomato puree
• 2 tablespoons hoisin sauce
• 1 teaspoon ground bean sauce
• 2 tablespoons fresh orange juice
• 2 tablespoons peanut oil
• 2 tablespoons sugar
• ½ tablespoon five-spice powder
• 1 tablespoon salt
• 1 teaspoon fresh ground pepper
• ½ tablespoon paprika
• 1 pound pork rib
Preparation:
1. In a large bowl, add all ingredients except for pork ribs and mix well.
2. Add the pork ribs and coat with mixture generously.
3. Cover the bowl and refrigerate to marinate for about 4-5 hours.
4. Preheat the oven to 325 degrees F.
5. Remove the ribs from the bowl and reserve the marinade.
6. Arrange the ribs onto a baking sheet.
7. Bake for about 35-40 minutes.

8. Flip the ribs and coat with the reserved marinade evenly.
9. Bake for about 10-15 minutes.
10. Serve hot
Serving Suggestions: Serve with the garnishing of scallion and sesame seeds.
Variation Tip: Adjust the ratio of sauces according to your choice.
Nutritional Information per Serving:
Calories: 953 | Fat: 54.7g|Sat Fat: 16.8g|Carbohydrates: 53.6g|Fiber: 2.1g|Sugar: 45g|Protein: 62.6g

Chinese Roasted Pork Pieces (Char Siu)

Prep Time: 15 minutes
Cook Time: 50 minutes
Servings: 3
Ingredients:
• 2 tablespoons honey
• 2 tablespoons dark soy sauce
• 2 tablespoons hoisin sauce
• 1 tablespoon sweet rice cooking wine
• 1 whole star anise pod, crushed
• Pinch of Chinese five-spice powder
• 1 (1 pound) boneless pork loin roast
Preparation:
1. In a microwave-safe bowl, add all the ingredients except the pork and mix until well combined.
2. Microwave on 60 percent power for about 20-25 seconds.
3. Stir the mixture well and transfer into a large resealable plastic bag alongside the pork loin.
4. Seal the bag and shake to coat well.
5. Refrigerate for about 4-12 hours.
6. Preheat grill for medium heat. Lightly grease the grill grate.
7. Remove pork roast from the bag and wrap in a piece of foil tightly.
8. Place the wrapped pork onto the grill and cook for about 50 minutes.
9. Remove from the grill and place the pork loin onto a cutting board for about 10 minutes before slicing.
10. With a sharp knife, cut into desired sized slices and serve.
Serving Suggestions: Serve with steamed green beans.
Variation Tip: Don't trim any excess fat from pork for better taste.
Nutritional Information per Serving:
Calories: 296 | Fat: 5.7g|Sat Fat: 1.8g|Carbohydrates: 19.4g|Fiber: 0.4g|Sugar: 15.9g|Protein: 40.6g

Ginger Beef with Carrot

Prep Time: 25 minutes.
Cook Time: 20 minutes.
Serves:4
Ingredients:
- ¾ cup corn-starch
- ½ cup water
- 2 eggs
- 1 pound flank steak, cut into thin strips
- ½ cup canola oil, or as needed
- 1 large carrot, cut into matchstick-size pieces
- 1 green bell pepper, cut into matchstick-size pieces
- 1 red bell pepper, cut into matchstick-size pieces
- 3 green onions, chopped
- ¼ cup minced fresh ginger root
- 5 garlic cloves, minced
- ½ cup white sugar
- ¼ cup rice vinegar
- 3 tablespoons soy sauce
- 1 tablespoon sesame oil
- 1 tablespoon red pepper flakes, or to taste

Preparation:
1. Place corn-starch in large bowl; Gradually stir in water until smooth. Beat eggs with corn-starch mixture; Put the beef strips in the dough to brush it.
2. Pour canola oil into a 1-inch-deep wok; Heat the oil over high heat until hot but not steaming. Place ¼ of the meat strips in hot oil; Bands separated with a fork. Cook, stirring frequently, until toppings are crispy and golden, about 3 minutes. Remove the meat on paper towels to drain it; repeat with the rest of the meat.
3. Drain all but 1 tablespoon of oil; Boil and stir carrots, green peppers, red peppers, green onions, ginger and garlic over high heat until lightly browned but still crisp, about 3 minutes.
4. Combine the sugar, rice vinegar, soy sauce, sesame oil and paprika in a small bowl. Pour the sauce mixture over the vegetables in the wok; Bring the mixture to a boil. Mix the meat again with the vegetable mixture; cook and stir until heated through, about 3 minutes.

Serving Suggestion: Serve the Ginger Beef with Carrot with salad or rice.
Variation Tip: Add about ¼ cup of teriyaki sauce as a variation.
Nutritional Information Per Serving:
Calories 768 | Fat 43g |Sodium 908mg | Carbs 57g | Fiber 2.5g | Sugar 29.9g | Protein 36.4g

Orange Beef with Broccoli

Prep Time: 20 minutes.
Cook Time: 15 minutes.
Serves:6
Ingredients:
- 1½ pounds beef top sirloin, thinly sliced
- ⅓ cup white sugar
- ⅓ cup rice wine vinegar
- 2 tablespoons frozen orange juice concentrate
- 1 teaspoon salt
- 1 tablespoon soy sauce
- 1 cup long grain rice
- 2 cups water
- ¼ cup corn-starch
- 2 teaspoons orange zest
- 3 tablespoons grated fresh ginger
- 1 ½ tablespoons minced garlic
- 8 broccoli florets, lightly steamed or blanched
- 2 cups oil for frying

Preparation:
1. Place the meat strips in a single layer on a paper towel lined baking sheet. Leave to dry in the refrigerator for 30 minutes. In a small bowl, combine the sugar, rice vinegar, orange juice concentrate, salt and soy sauce. Put aside.
2. Meanwhile, combine the rice and water in a medium saucepan. Bring to a boil, then reduce the heat to medium-low and simmer for 20 minutes, or until the rice is tender. If necessary, add more water last.
3. Heat the oil in a wok over medium heat. Throw in the corn-starch beef to coat it. Fry in hot oil in small portions until crispy and golden; put aside. Drain all the oil from the wok except for a tablespoon.
4. Add the orange zest, ginger and garlic to the remaining oil and sauté briefly until fragrant. Pour the soy sauce mixture into the wok, bring to a boil and cook for about 5 minutes thick and syrupy.
5. Add the meat and heat to coat. Serve immediately over steamed rice and garnish with broccoli.

Serving Suggestion: Serve the Orange Beef with Broccoli with rice.
Variation Tip: Use brown rice.
Nutritional Information Per Serving:
Calories 298 | Fat 6.1g |Sodium 560mg | Carbs 50.7g | Fiber 0.9g | Sugar 11.9g | Protein 9.9g

Chinese Grilled Hoisin Beef

Prep Time: 10 minutes.
Cook Time: 10 minutes.
Serves:4
Ingredients:
• 1 (1 pound) beef skirt steak
• ⅓ cup hoisin sauce
• 3 tablespoons Chinese vinegar
• 1 tablespoon soy sauce
• 2 teaspoons hot sauce
• 2 teaspoons sesame oil
• 1 tablespoon grated fresh ginger root
• 4 cloves garlic, finely minced
• 1 tablespoon packed brown sugar
• 1 teaspoon salt
• ½ teaspoon freshly ground black pepper
• 1 green onion, light parts only, minced
• Toasted sesame seeds
Preparation:
1. Combine hoisin sauce, vinegar, soy sauce, hot sauce, sesame oil, grated ginger, garlic, brown sugar, salt and pepper in a large mixing bowl.
2. Cut the rock steak crosswise into 4-5 smaller pieces. Place the steak in the marinade and toss until all the pieces are evenly coated. Cover with plastic wrap. Fresh; marinate for at least 2 hours and up to 12 hours.
3. Cover a baking sheet with paper towel. Place the pieces of meat on paper towels and wipe off some of the marinade.
4. Preheat an outdoor grill on high heat and lightly grease the grill.
5. Transfer the pieces of meat to the grill. Cook over medium heat for 4 to 5 minutes per side. An instant-read thermometer inserted in the center should read between 130 to 135 degrees F (approximately 54 degrees C). Thinner parts can be finished earlier. Transfer the steak to a hot plate. Leave to rest for a few minutes.
6. Transfer the steak to a hot dish and pour the juice accumulated over the rock steak. Sprinkle with sesame seeds and sliced spring onions.
Serving Suggestion: Serve the Chinese Grilled Hoisin Beef with savory coconut rice.
Variation Tip: Use sherry vinegar if not found Chinese vinegar.
Nutritional Information Per Serving:
Calories 331 | Fat 17.2g |Sodium 1360mg | Carbs 12.7g | Fiber 1.5g | Sugar 8.9g | Protein 31.4g

Stir-fried Beef with Snow Peas

Prep Time: 10 minutes
Cook Time: 10 minutes
Servings: 3
Ingredients:
For marinade:
• 2 teaspoons Chinese rice wine
• 1½ teaspoons dark soy sauce
• 1½ teaspoons light soy sauce
• ½ teaspoon sesame oil
• 2 teaspoons corn-starch
• 1 teaspoon sugar
• Freshly ground black pepper, to taste
• ¾ pound flank steak, cut into thin strips
For cooking:
• 2 tablespoons canola oil, divided
• 6 ounces snow peas, trimmed
• 1½ teaspoons garlic, minced
• Salt, to taste
• 1-2 tablespoons rice wine
Preparation:
1. For marinade: in a bowl, add all ingredients except for steak strips and mix until well combined.
2. Add the steak strips and coat with marinade generously.
3. Set aside for about 15 minutes.
4. In a heavy-bottomed skillet, heat 2 tablespoons of oil over medium-high heat and sear the steak strips with marinade for about 4-6 minutes or until desired doneness.
5. With a slotted spoon, transfer the steak strips onto a plate.
6. In the same skillet, heat the remaining oil over medium heat and stir fry the snow peas and garlic for about 2 minutes.
7. Stir in the cooked steak strips, wine and salt and stir fry for about 1-2 minutes.
8. Serve hot.
Serving Suggestions: Serve with the garnishing of sesame seeds.
Variation Tip: For extra flavor, try to use pre-seasoned oil while searing the steak strips.
Nutritional Information per Serving:
Calories: 357 | Fat: 19.7g|Sat Fat: 4.7g|Carbohydrates: 10g|Fiber: 1.7g|Sugar: 5g|Protein: 33.7g

Marinated Beef with Sesame Seeds

Prep Time: 15 minutes plus 15 minutes for marinating.
Cook Time: 10 minutes.
Serves: 4
Ingredients:
• ½ pound flank steak
• ½ red bell pepper
• ½ green bell pepper
• 1 cup mung bean sprouts
• 1 stalk celery
Marinade:
• 4 teaspoons liquid honey
• 3 tablespoons soy sauce
• 1 tablespoon water
• 1 green onion (chopped)
• 2 teaspoons corn-starch
Sauce:
• 1 tablespoon oyster sauce
• ¼ cup low-sodium chicken broth
• 1 teaspoon granulated sugar
Other:
• 1 clove garlic
• 2 slices ginger
• 1 teaspoon corn-starch mixed with 4 teaspoons water
• 3 tablespoons white sesame seeds (toasted)
• 4 tablespoons oil for stir-frying
Preparation:
1. Wash and drain the vegetables. Remove the stems and seeds from the peppers and cut them into thin strips. Rinse the mung bean sprouts well and let them drain. Rack the celery and cut it diagonally into thin strips.
2. Cut the rock steak into thin strips along the fibres. Mix with the marinade ingredients, add the corn-starch last.
3. Marinate the steak for 15 minutes. Mix the ingredients for the sauce and set aside.
4. Heat the wok over medium heat. Put 2 tablespoons of oil in the heated wok. When the oil is ready, add the meat. Fry briefly, then fry almost cooked. Take out of the wok.
5. Clean the wok if necessary. Add 2 tablespoons of oil. Add garlic and ginger and sauté briefly until fragrant (about 30 seconds).
6. Add the green peppers and celery. Sauté briefly and add the red pepper. Slide the vegetables against the sides of the wok.
7. Place the sauce in the middle of the wok. Heat briefly, then add the corn-starch and water porridge while stirring to thicken. Return the steak to the wok. Add the mung bean sprouts. Mix everything.
8. Sprinkle with sesame seeds before serving
Serving Suggestion: Serve the Marinated Beef with Sesame Seeds with salad.
Variation Tip: Use white granulated sugar if not access Chinese rock sugar.
Nutritional Information Per Serving:
Calories 227 | Fat 17.2g |Sodium 560mg | Carbs 12.7g | Fiber 0.6g | Sugar 1.9g | Protein 9g

Mongolian Beef with Sesame Seeds

Prep Time: 10 minutes
Cook Time: 10 minutes
Servings: 4
Ingredients:
• 1 pound flank steak, cut into thin slices against the grain
• 2 teaspoons corn-starch
• Salt, to taste
• ¼ cup avocado oil
• 1 (1-inch) piece fresh ginger, grated
• 4 garlic cloves, minced
• ½ teaspoon red pepper flakes, crushed
• ¼ cup water
• ⅓ cup low-sodium soy sauce
• 1 teaspoon fish sauce
• 3 scallions, sliced
• 1 teaspoon sesame seeds
Preparation:
1. In a bowl, add the steak slices, corn-starch and salt and toss to coat well.
2. In a larger skillet, heat oil over medium-high heat and cook the steak slices for about 1½ minutes per side.
3. With a slotted spoon, transfer the steak slices onto a plate.
4. Drain the oil from the skillet but leaving about 1 tablespoon inside.
5. In the same skillet, add the ginger, garlic and red pepper flakes and sauté for about 1 minute.
6. Add the water, soy sauce and fish sauce and stir to combine well.
7. Stir in the cooked steak slices and simmer for about 3 minutes.
8. Stir in the scallions and simmer for about 2 minutes.
9. Remove from the heat and serve hot with the garnishing of sesame seeds.
Serving Suggestions: Serve over rice.
Variation Tip: Cut the beef into uniform-sized slices.
Nutritional Information per Serving:
Calories: 269 | Fat: 11.7g|Sat Fat: 4.4g|Carbohydrates: 6.5g|Fiber: 1.3g|Sugar: 1.8g|Protein: 33.8g

Tasty Beef and Vegetables

Prep Time: 10 minutes.
Cook Time: 30 minutes.
Serves:4
Ingredients:
- 8 ounces beef filet, cut into ½ inch strips
- 2 tablespoons vegetable oil
- 1 onion, chopped
- 1 clove garlic, minced
- 1 teaspoon chopped fresh ginger root
- 1 green bell pepper, chopped
- 1 carrot, chopped
- 1 (10.5 ounce) can beef broth
- 1 tablespoon corn-starch
- 1 teaspoon white sugar
- 1 tablespoon soy sauce
- 1 tablespoon oyster sauce
- salt and pepper to taste

Preparation:
1. In a large skillet over medium heat, brown the meat slices in the oil for 5 minutes or until golden brown. Add the onion, garlic and ginger and sauté for another 5 minutes. Then add the green pepper, carrot and beef broth. Reduce the heat to low and bring to a boil.
2. Meanwhile, combine the cornmeal, sugar, soy sauce and oyster sauce in a separate small bowl. Mix well until a smooth paste form. Slowly add it to the simmering meat and vegetables, stir well and simmer to the desired thickness. Season to taste with salt and pepper.
Serving Suggestion: Serve the Tasty Beef and Vegetables with rice.
Variation Tip: Use honey intends of using white sugar.
Nutritional Information Per Serving:
Calories 231 | Fat 12.2g |Sodium 536mg | Carbs 10.7g | Fiber 1.5g | Sugar 4.9g | Protein 19g

Chinese Pepper Steak with Tomato

Prep Time: 15 minutes.
Cook Time: 15 minutes.
Serves:4
Ingredients:

- 1 pound beef top sirloin steak
- ¼ cup soy sauce
- 2 tablespoons white sugar
- 2 tablespoons corn-starch
- ½ teaspoon ground ginger
- 3 tablespoons vegetable oil, divided
- 1 red onion, cut into 1-inch squares
- 1 green bell pepper, cut into 1-inch squares
- 2 tomatoes, cut into wedges

Preparation:
1. Cut the steak into ½-inch-thick slices along the grain.
2. Combine soy sauce, sugar, corn-starch and ginger in a bowl until the sugar is dissolved and the mixture is smooth. Place the steak slices in the marinade and stir until well covered.
3. Heat 1 tablespoon of vegetable oil in a wok or large skillet over medium heat and place ⅓ of the steak strips in the hot oil. Cook, stirring, until the meat is golden, about 3 minutes, and remove the meat from the wok into a bowl. Repeat the process two more times with the remaining meat, keeping the meat cooked.
4. Return all the cooked meat to the hot wok and add the onion. Mix meat and onion until onion begins to soften, about 2 minutes, then add green pepper.
5. Boil and stir the mixture until the pepper turns light green and begins to soften, about 2 minutes, then add the tomatoes, stir everything and serve.
Serving Suggestion: Serve the Chinese Pepper Steak with Tomato with rice.
Variation Tip: Use honey if not want to use white sugar.
Nutritional Information Per Serving:
Calories 379 | Fat 17.2g |Sodium 978mg | Carbs 18.7g | Fiber 1.5g | Sugar 10.9g | Protein 36.4g

Hoisin Mongolian Beef

Prep Time: 15 minutes.
Cook Time: 6 minutes.
Serves:4
Ingredients:
- ¼ cup soy sauce
- 1 tablespoon hoisin sauce
- 1 tablespoon sesame oil
- 2 teaspoons white sugar
- 1 tablespoon minced garlic
- 1 tablespoon red pepper flakes (Optional)
- 1-pound beef flank steak, thinly sliced
- 1 tablespoon peanut oil
- 2 large green onions, thinly sliced

Preparation:
1. Whisk soy sauce, hoisin sauce, sesame oil, sugar, garlic and paprika flakes in a bowl. Put the meat in

the marinade, cover and refrigerate for 1 hour to overnight.

2. Heat the peanut oil in a wok or large non-stick skillet over high heat. Add the green onions and cook 5 to 10 seconds before adding the meat. Cook and stir until meat is no longer pink and brown, about 5 minutes.

Serving Suggestion: Serve the Hoisin Mongolian Beef with rice.

Variation Tip: Use honey if not want to use white sugar.

Nutritional Information Per Serving:
Calories 307 | Fat 27.2g |Sodium 1560mg | Carbs 2.7g | Fiber 0.5g | Sugar 1.9g | Protein 34.4g

Pan-fried Dumplings

Prep Time: 50 minutes.
Cook Time: 10 minutes.
Serves:12
Ingredients:
• 1-pound raw shrimp, peeled and deveined
• 4 pounds ground beef
• 1 tablespoon minced fresh ginger root
• 1 shallot, minced
• 1 bunch green onions, chopped
• 3 leaves napa cabbage, chopped
• 2 tablespoons soy sauce
• 1 teaspoon Asian (toasted) sesame oil
• salt and white pepper to taste
• 1 pinch white sugar
• 1 (10 ounce) package round gyoza/potsticker wrappers
• vegetable oil
• ¼ cup water
Preparation:
1. Place the shrimp in the bowl of a food processor and mix until finely ground. Store in a large bowl. Process the minced meat in batches until finely ground and store it with the shrimp. Mix the shrimp and minced meat with the ginger, shallots, spring onions, napa cabbage, soy sauce, sesame oil, salt, pepper and white sugar and mix the ingredients well.
2. To fill the jar stickers, place a wrapper in front of you on a work surface and place a small teaspoon of filler in the middle. Moisten the edges of the packaging with a damp finger. Fold the dough into a crescent shape, enclose the filling, press it down and close it to remove excess air and seal the edges well. It is good to make several small folds in the top half of the wrapper to give it a traditional look before sealing the filling. Cool the filled wraps on a parchment-lined baking sheet while you finish filling and sealing the potstickers.
3. Heat the oil in a large non-stick skillet with a lid over medium heat. Place the pot sticker flat side

down in the hot oil without lumpiness and fry for 1 to 2 minutes until the bottom is golden. Turn the meatballs over and pour the water over them. Cover the pot with a lid and let the meatballs steam until the water has almost evaporated and the meatballs again sauté in the oil for 5-7 minutes. Cover the pot and let the stickers boil until all the water has evaporated and the film has shrunk well on the filling, another 2-3 minutes.

Serving Suggestion: Serve the Pan-fried Dumplings with salad or noodles.

Variation Tip: This recipe makes a large batch of filling, enough for several packages of dumpling wrappers.

Nutritional Information Per Serving:
Calories 342 | Fat 11.2g |Sodium 343mg | Carbs 1.1g | Fiber 0.1g | Sugar 1.0g | Protein 54.4g

Chinese Braised Short Ribs

Prep Time: 10 minutes
Cook Time: 2 hours 20 minutes
Servings: 4
Ingredients:
• 2 tablespoons vegetable oil
• 4 large bone-in beef short ribs
• Salt and freshly ground black pepper, to taste
• 1 medium red onion, chopped
• 1 (3-inch) piece fresh ginger, grated
• 1 cup water
• ½ cup unseasoned rice wine vinegar
• ½ cup soy sauce
• 2 tablespoons Sriracha
• 2 tablespoons brown sugar
• 2 tablespoons scallion greens, chopped
• 1 teaspoon sesame seeds
Preparation:
1. In a Dutch oven, melt the butter over medium-high heat and cook the short ribs with a little salt and black pepper for about 6-7 minutes per side.
2. With a slotted spoon, transfer the short ribs onto a plate.
3. In the same pan, add the onion and ginger over medium heat and sauté for about 3 minutes.
4. Add the water, vinegar, soy sauce, Sriracha and brown sugar and stir to combine.
5. Place the cooked short ribs in the pan in a single layer.
6. Cover the pan and transfer into the oven.
7. Bake for about 30 minutes.
8. Remove from the oven and with tongs, flip the short ribs.

9. Cover the pan and again, transfer into the oven.
10. Bake for about 70 minutes, flipping the short ribs after every 30 minutes.
11. Remove from the oven and with tongs, transfer the short ribs onto a platter.
12. With a piece of foil, cover the short ribs to keep warm.
13. Place the pan with the juices over medium-high heat and bring to a boil.
14. Cook for about 8-12 minutes, stirring occasionally.
15. Through a strainer, strain the cooking juice into a heatproof bowl, discarding the solids.
16. Set the bowl aside until fat rises to the top.
17. With a spoon, remove the fat from the top.
18. Place the strained cooking juice over short ribs and serve with the garnishing of scallion greens and sesame seeds.

Serving Suggestions: Serve alongside the steamed Bok choy.
Variation Tip: Remove only the thickest layers of external fat. from ribs.
Nutritional Information per Serving:
Calories: 728 | Fat: 32.9g|Sat Fat: 11.2g|Carbohydrates: 13.2g|Fiber: 1.4g|Sugar: 6.2g|Protein: 84.6g

Hot Beef with Broccoli

Prep Time: 15 minutes.
Cook Time: 10 minutes.
Serves:4
Ingredients:
• ¾ pound boneless tender beef steak, rib eye, sirloin or flank
• 1 tablespoon corn-starch
• 3 tablespoons soy sauce, divided
• 1 large clove garlic, minced
• ½ teaspoon sugar
• 1-pound fresh broccoli, trimmed
• 4 teaspoons corn-starch
• ½ teaspoon crushed red pepper
• 3 tablespoons vegetable oil, divided
• 1 medium onion, thinly sliced
• 2 teaspoons seasoned rice vinegar
Preparation:
1. Cut the meat into thin slices in the direction of the grain. Mix 1 tablespoon each corn-starch and garlic, sugar, and soy sauce in a medium bowl; add the beef. Leave to rest for 10 minutes.
2. Meanwhile, remove the broccoli flowers; Cut into bite-sized pieces. Peel the stems; Cut diagonally into thin slices.
3. Combine 1 cup of water with the remaining 2 tablespoons. Place the remaining soy sauce, 4 teaspoons of corn-starch and crushed red peppers in a small bowl. Put aside.

4. Heat 1 tablespoon of oil in a hot wok or large skillet over high heat. Add the meat and sauté for 1 minute; remove.
5. Heat the remaining 2 tablespoons of oil in the same pan. Add broccoli and onion; Fry for 2 minutes. Sprinkle 1 tablespoon of water on vegetables; cover and cook for 2 minutes, stirring occasionally.
6. Add meat mixture and soy sauce; cook and stir until sauce boils and thickens. Remove the stove; add the vinegar to season and serve.

Serving Suggestion: Serve the Hot Beef with Broccoli with rice or noodles.
Variation Tip: Use apple cider vinegar if not finding rice vinegar.
Nutritional Information Per Serving:
Calories 311 | Fat 15.9g |Sodium 898mg | Carbs 12.7g | Fiber 3.5g | Sugar 3.9g | Protein 29.4g

Sesame Beef with Broccoli

Prep Time: 15 minutes
Cook Time: 20 minutes
Servings: 4
Ingredients:
• 14 ounces sirloin steak, trimmed and cut into thin strips
• Freshly ground black pepper, to taste
• 2 tablespoons vegetable oil, divided
• 1 small yellow onion, chopped
• 2 garlic cloves, minced
• 1 Serrano pepper, seeded and chopped finely
• 3 cups broccoli florets
• 3 tablespoons low-sodium soy sauce
• 2 tablespoons fresh lime juice
• 1 teaspoon sesame seeds
Preparation:
1. Season steak with black pepper.
2. In a large skillet, heat 1 tablespoon of the oil over medium heat and cook the steak for about 6-8 minutes or until browned from all sides.
3. With a slotted spoon, transfer the steak onto a plate.
4. In the same skillet, heat the remaining oil and sauté onion for about 3-4 minutes.
5. Add the garlic and Serrano pepper and sauté for about 1 minute.
6. Add broccoli and stir fry for about 2-3 minutes.
7. Stir in cooked beef, soy sauce and lime juice and cook for about 3-4 minutes.
8. Serve hot with the garnishing of sesame seeds.
Serving Suggestions: Serve with boiled jasmine rice.
Variation Tip: Try to use small-sized broccoli florets.
Nutritional Information per Serving:
Calories: 286 | Fat: 13.6g|Sat Fat: 3.8g|Carbohydrates: 7.8g|Fiber: 2.3g|Sugar: 2.7g|Protein: 33.2g

Fire Beef

Prep Time: 15 minutes plus 2 hours for marinating.
Cook Time: 05 minutes.
Serves: 4
Ingredients:
- ½ cup soy sauce
- 1 tablespoon sesame oil
- 2 tablespoons brown sugar
- 3 cloves garlic, crushed
- 1 large red onion, chopped
- ground black pepper to taste
- 1 teaspoon red pepper flakes
- 2 tablespoons sesame seeds
- 2 leeks, chopped
- 1 small carrot, chopped
- 1-pound beef round steak, sliced paper thin

Preparation:
1. In a large bowl, combine soy sauce, sesame oil, brown sugar, garlic and red onion together. Add black pepper, red pepper flakes, sesame seeds, leek and carrot. Mix meat by hand to ensure even coverage. Cover and marinate for at least 2 hours or overnight.
2. Brush the bottom half of a wok with cooking oil and heat over medium to high heat. Add all the meat and marinade at once and cook, stirring constantly. The meat will cook after a few minutes. Remove from the heat and serve with rice or pasta. For Korean-style fiery meat, roll the meat mixture in a leaf of red lettuce.

Serving Suggestion: Serve the Fire Beef with salad.
Variation Tip: Use garlic powder.
Nutritional Information Per Serving:
Calories 425 | Fat 27.2g |Sodium 1560mg | Carbs 2.7g | Fiber 0.5g | Sugar 1.9g | Protein 34.4g

Beef and Veggies Dumplings

Prep Time: 20 minutes
Cook Time: 10 minutes
Servings: 10
Ingredients:
- 1½ pounds ground beef
- 2 cups Chinese cabbage, shredded
- 1 carrot, peeled and shredded
- 1 onion, minced
- 1 egg
- 1 tablespoon vegetable oil
- 1 tablespoon soy sauce

- 1 teaspoon sugar
- 1 teaspoon salt
- 1 (14-ounce) package wonton wrappers

Preparation:
1. For filling: in a large bowl, add the beef, cabbage, carrot, onion, egg, oil, soy sauce, sugar and salt and mix until well combined.
2. Arrange 1 wonton wrapper onto a smooth surface.
3. Place about 1 teaspoon of the filling in the center of the wrapper.
4. With wet fingers, moisten the edges of the wrapper and then fold in half.
5. With your fingers, pinch the edges together to seal the filling.
6. Repeat with remaining wonton wrappers and filling.
7. In a large pan of boiling water, cook the dumplings in 2 batches for about 5 minutes, stirring occasionally.
8. With a slotted spoon, transfer the dumplings onto a paper towel-lined plate to drain.

Serving Suggestions: Serve with seasoned so sauce.
Variation Tip: You can also cook the dumplings in chicken broth.
Nutritional Information per Serving:
Calories: 273 | Fat: 6.7g|Sat Fat: 2.1g|Carbohydrates: 26g|Fiber: 1.5g|Sugar: 1.7g|Protein: 25.5g

Chinese Stir-fried Beef & Green Beans

Prep Time: 15 minutes
Cook Time: 22 minutes
Servings: 3
Ingredients:
- 1 tablespoon dark soy sauce
- 1 teaspoon light soy sauce
- ½ teaspoon granulated sugar
- 4 tablespoons peanut oil, divided
- ¾ pound green beans, trimmed and cut into 2-inch-long pieces
- 2 medium scallions, chopped finely
- 1 tablespoon fresh ginger, chopped finely
- 1 tablespoon garlic, chopped finely
- 1 teaspoon chile paste
- ¾ pound flank steak, cut into thin strips
- 1 tablespoon Chinese rice wine
- Salt and freshly ground black pepper, to taste
- ½ teaspoon sesame oil

Preparation:
1. In a small bowl, add the soy sauces and sugar and mix well. Set aside.
2. In a skillet, heat 2 tablespoons of peanut oil over medium heat and stir fry the green beans for about 7-10 minutes.

3. With a slotted spoon, transfer the green beans onto a plate.
4. In the same skillet, heat the remaining oil over high heat and stir fry the scallions, ginger and garlic for about 30 seconds.
5. Stir in the chile paste and stir fry for about 30 seconds.
6. Stir in the steak strips and cook for about 1 minute, without stirring.
7. Stir in the wine and stir fry for about 4-6 minutes.
8. Stir in the sauce mixture and stir fry for about 1-2 minutes.
9. Stir in the green beans, salt and black pepper and cook for about 1-2 minutes.
10. Remove from the heat and stir in the sesame oil.
11. Serve hot.
Serving Suggestions: Serve with the garnishing of sesame seeds.
Variation Tip: Choose a flank steak that is as uniform as possible in its thickness.
Nutritional Information per Serving:
Calories: 357 | Fat: 19.7g|Sat Fat: 12.8g|Carbohydrates: 10g|Fiber: 1.7g|Sugar: 5g|Protein: 33.7g

Crispy Beef Chili with Pepper

Prep Time: 10 minutes
Cook Time: 15 minutes
Servings: 3
Ingredients:
• ¾ pound sirloin steaks, cut into thin strips
• 1 small egg
• 4 tablespoons corn flour
• Salt, to taste
• ¼ teaspoon ground white pepper
• ¼ teaspoon freshly ground black pepper
• 4½ tablespoons sunflower oil, divided
• 1 medium onion, sliced into thin strips
• 3 garlic cloves, minced
• 1 teaspoon fresh ginger, minced
• 1 red chili, sliced finely
• 3 tablespoons dark soy sauce
• 2 tablespoons sweet chili sauce
• 2 tablespoons rice vinegar
• 2 tablespoons tomato puree
• 2 tablespoons tomato ketchup
• 6 tablespoons caster sugar
• 2-3 tablespoons scallion greens, sliced
Preparation:
1. In a bowl, add the steak strips, egg, corn flour, salt, and white pepper and black pepper and mix until well combined.
2. In a large skillet, heat 3 tablespoons of the oil over a high heat and sear the steak slices for about 5-6 minutes or until dark brown and crispy, stirring 3-4 stirs times.
3. With a slotted spoon, transfer the steak slices onto a paper towel-lined plate to drain excess oil.

4. In the same skillet, heat the remaining oil over medium heat and sauté the onion for about 2 minutes.
5. Add in the garlic, ginger and red chili and sauté for about 1 minute.
6. Stir in the remaining ingredients except for scallion greens and stir to combine.
7. Increase the heat to medium-high and cook for about 2 minutes, stirring frequently.
8. Add in the cooked steak strips and cook for about 1-2 minutes, stirring frequently.
9. Serve hot with the garnishing of scallion greens.
Serving Suggestions: Serve with cooked noodles.
Variation Tip: If you don't like your dish too hot, remove the seeds from red chili.
Nutritional Information per Serving:
Calories: 592 | Fat: 29.9g|Sat Fat: 5.2g|Carbohydrates: 41.7g|Fiber: 2.2g|Sugar: 29g|Protein: 38.8g

Mongolian Meatballs with Sesame Seeds

Prep Time: 15 minutes
Cook Time: 15 minutes
Servings: 4
Ingredients:
For meatballs:
• ½ cup panko breadcrumbs
• 1 large egg
• ½ cup scallion (white pat), sliced thinly
• 1 tablespoon garlic, minced
• 1 tablespoon low-sodium soy sauce
• ¼ teaspoon red pepper flakes, crushed
• ¼ teaspoon freshly ground white pepper
• Salt, to taste
• 1 pound ground beef
For sauce:
• ½ cup water
• ¼ cup low-sodium soy sauce
• 1 tablespoon hoisin sauce
• 1 tablespoon oyster sauce
• 2 teaspoons sesame oil
• 2 teaspoons fresh ginger, grated
• 4 garlic cloves, grated
• ⅓ cup brown sugar
• ⅛ teaspoon red pepper flakes, crushed
• ⅛ teaspoon ground white pepper
For garnishing:
• 2-3 tablespoons scallion greens, chopped
• 2 teaspoons sesame seeds, toasted
Preparation:
1. Preheat the oven to 450 degrees F. Arrange a rack in the center position of oven. Line a baking sheet with parchment paper.
2. For meatballs: in a large bowl, add all ingredients except for beef and mix until well combined.

3. Add the ground beef and mix until just combined.
4. With about 1½ tablespoon of the mixture, make meatballs.
5. Arrange the meatballs onto the prepared baking sheet in a single layer.
6. Bake for about 8-10 minutes or until cooked through.
7. Meanwhile, for sauce: in a large skillet, add all ingredients over medium-high heat and bring to a boil, stirring frequently.
8. Reduce the heat to low and simmer for about 5-6 minutes, stirring frequently.
9. Remove the meatballs from oven and add into the skillet of sauce.
10. Cook for about 1-2 minutes, tossing occasionally.
11. Serve hot with the garnishing of scallion greens and sesame seeds.
Serving Suggestions: Serve with steamed rice.
Variation Tip: To avoid tough meatballs, don't overmix the ground beef with the remaining ingredients.
Nutritional Information per Serving:
Calories: 384 | Fat: 12.5g|Sat Fat: 3.9g|Carbohydrates: 30.9g|Fiber: 0.9g|Sugar: 14.6g|Protein: 38.7g

Sauced Beef ,Cabbage, and Carrot

Prep Time: 15 minutes
Cook Time: 17 minutes
Servings: 6
Ingredients:
For sauce:
• 3 tablespoons low-sodium soy sauce
• 2 tablespoons oyster sauce
• 1 tablespoon hoisin sauce
• 1 tablespoon dark soy sauce
• 2 teaspoons Chinese cooking wine
• 1 teaspoon sesame oil
• 1 teaspoon white granulated sugar
For beef mixture:
• 1 tablespoon vegetable oil
• 1 small onion, sliced
• 1 teaspoon fresh ginger, minced
• 4 garlic cloves, minced
• 1-pound lean ground beef
• 8 cups cabbage, shredded
• 1 large carrot, peeled and shredded
• Salt and freshly ground black pepper, to taste
Preparation:
1. For sauce: in a bowl, add all ingredient and beat until sugar is dissolved. Set aside.
2. In a large skillet, heat the oil over medium-high heat and sauté the onion for about 3 minutes.
3. Add in the ginger and garlic and sauté for about 30 seconds.

4. Add the beef and cook for about 5 minutes, breaking up the meat with a wooden spoon frequently.
5. Stir in half of the sauce and stir to combine.
6. Add the cabbage and carrots and cook for about 5-6 minutes, stirring occasionally.
7. Stir in the remaining sauce, salt and black pepper and cook for about 1-2 minutes, stirring frequently.
8. Serve it.
Serving Suggestions: Serve with the garnishing of scallion.
Variation Tip: You can add sriracha for heat.
Nutritional Information per Serving:
Calories: 219 | Fat: 8g|Sat Fat: 2.4g|Carbohydrates: 11.3g|Fiber: 3.1g|Sugar: 6.1g|Protein: 25.3g

Sautéed Steak with Pepper

Prep Time: 10 minutes
Cook Time: 25 minutes
Servings: 5
Ingredients:
• 1 tablespoon corn flour
• 1½ tablespoons water
• 2 tablespoons sesame oil
• 2 garlic cloves, minced
• 1½ pounds beef steak, cut into strips
• 1 red bell pepper, seeded and julienned
• 1 green bell pepper, seeded and julienned
• 1 cup fresh mushrooms, sliced
• ¾ cup beef broth
• ¼ cup light soy sauce
• 2 teaspoons sugar
• ½ teaspoon salt
• ½ teaspoon ground white pepper
Preparation:
1. In a small bowl, dissolve corn flour in water. Set aside.
2. In a large skillet, heat the oil over medium heat and sauté the garlic for about 1 minute.
3. Add steak strips and cook for about 6-8 minutes, stirring frequently.
4. With a slotted spoon, transfer the steak strips onto a plate.
5. In the same skillet, add the bell peppers and mushrooms and cook for about 5-6 minutes.
6. Add broth, soy sauce, sugar, salt and black pepper and cook for about 7-8 minutes.
7. Add the cooked steak strips and stir to combine.
8. Add the corn flour mixture and cook for 2-3 minutes, stirring continuously.
9. Serve hot.
Serving Suggestions: Serve with hot cooked rice.
Variation Tip: You can use mushrooms of your choice.
Nutritional Information per Serving:
Calories: 345 | Fat: 14.4g|Sat Fat: 4g|Carbohydrates: 8.4g|Fiber: 1.1g|Sugar: 4.6g|Protein: 43.9g

Yummy Deep-fried Oysters

Prep Time: 30 minutes.
Cook Time: 15 minutes.
Serves:4
Ingredients:
For the deep-fried oysters:
• ½ pound shucked oysters(225g)
• 6 tablespoons all-purpose flour for the batter (plus ⅓ cup for dredging the oysters)
• ¼ teaspoon baking powder
• ⅛ teaspoon ground white pepper
• ⅛ teaspoon garlic powder
• ⅛ teaspoon onion powder
• ½ teaspoon salt
• 1 cup coconut oil (for frying)
• ¼ cup ice cold seltzer water
• ¼ teaspoon sesame oil
• Iceberg lettuce (shredded)
• ½ scallion (chopped, for garnish)
For the dipping sauce:
• ½ tablespoon ketchup
• ½ teaspoon soy sauce
• 1 tablespoons rice vinegar
• ⅛ teaspoon salt
• 1 tablespoons sugar
• ½ teaspoon corn-starch
Preparation:
1. Drain the peeled oysters from the plastic container and rinse thoroughly under cold water. Oysters are very delicate, so be careful when handling them. Put the oysters in a colander and let the excess water drain for at least 10 minutes.
2. Prepare the dough by mixing ¾ cup of flour, baking powder, white pepper, garlic powder, onion powder and salt until combined.
3. Heat the oil in a small (to save oil) but deep (to avoid splashing) saucepan to 350 degrees F. Check the temperature of the oil with a candy or oil thermometer to verify accuracy.
4. Just before you want to fry the oysters, add the cold seltzer; makes for a crispier oyster. Mix until your dough is smooth (a few small lumps here and there are fine). Then add the sesame oil.
5. Once the oysters are drained, gently dry each oyster with a paper towel and lightly dust each oyster with flour. I know it is tempting to dredge all the loose oysters at once, but it is best to dredge each oyster one at a time just before coating and frying them to make sure they are fully and evenly coated.
6. After dredging, dip each oyster in the paste so that it is completely covered. Carefully remove them from the dough; You can use the rim of the bowl to scrape off excess dough if needed.

7. You are now ready to fry the oysters. Check the oil temperature again with your thermometer. While frying, adjust the heat to maintain a temperature between 325 ° F and 350 ° F, as the oil will cool quickly if you put the breaded oysters in it and quickly reheat it during cooking.
8. Dip the oyster halfway into the oil and swirl it slowly for 2-3 seconds to allow the dough to cook a bit, then drop it into the oil. This process prevents the oyster from sticking to the bottom of the pot. Fry the oysters in portions, depending on the size of the pot and the amount of oil. For this recipe, we fry the oysters in servings of 3 or 4, depending on their size.
9. Use a slotted spoon to scoop up the golden oysters and transfer them to a metal refrigerator shelf to drain. Repeat until all the oysters are fried.
10. You can now prepare the dip. In a small saucepan, add the tomato sauce, soy sauce, rice vinegar, salt, sugar and corn-starch mixture and heat over low heat. You can adjust the taste by adding vinegar to make it more acidic, adding sugar if you like it sweeter, or adding more corn-starch and water if you like it thicker.
11. Better to serve them right away, but if you're like us at Chinese New Year, you cook a lot at once and it's inevitable that you won't eat them right away! Just before serving, you can heat the oil to 375 degrees F and drop the oysters in 3 or 4 at a time, fry them for 30 seconds or until crisp again. Alternatively, you can use a toaster to heat them at 400 ° F for 5 minutes.
12. Serve these fried oysters on a bed of iceberg lettuce and garnish with chopped chives. The dip should be served lukewarm, so reheat it if necessary.
Serving Suggestion: Serve the deep-fried oysters with rice.
Variation Tip: Use almond flour if not want to use all-purpose flour.
Nutritional Information Per Serving:
Calories 145 | Fat 8g |Sodium 294mg | Carbs 17g | Fiber 1g | Sugar 4g | Protein 2g

Classic Szechwan Shrimp

Prep Time: 10 minutes.
Cook Time: 10 minutes.
Serves:2
Ingredients:
• 2 tablespoons water
• 1 tablespoon ketchup
• ½ tablespoon soy sauce
• 1 teaspoon corn-starch
• ½ teaspoon honey
• ¼ teaspoon crushed red pepper

- ⅛ teaspoon ground ginger
- ½ tablespoon vegetable oil
- ⅛ cup sliced green onions
- 2 cloves garlic, minced
- 6 ounces cooked shrimp, tails removed

Preparation:
1. In a bowl, combine the water, tomato sauce, soy sauce, corn-starch, honey, crushed red pepper and ground ginger. Put aside.
2. Heat the oil in a large skillet over medium heat. Add the green onions and garlic; Cook for 30 seconds. Add the shrimp and toss to cover with oil. Add the sauce. Cook and stir until the sauce is bubbly and thick.

Serving Suggestion: Serve the Szechwan Shrimp with brown rice.

Variation Tip: Use maple syrup if not want honey.

Nutritional Information Per Serving:
Calories 158 | Fat 4.9g |Sodium 519mg | Carbs 7.8g | Fiber 0.4g | Sugar 3.4g | Protein 20.9g

Salmon and Anchovies with Tomato

Prep Time: 05 minutes.
Cook Time: 25 minutes.
Serves:6
Ingredients:
- 1-pound thin spaghetti
- 3 tablespoons olive oil
- 10 cloves garlic (thinly sliced)
- 4 anchovies (at a minimum; can use up to a whole can)
- ⅓ cup capers (roughly chopped)
- ¼ teaspoon crushed red pepper flakes
- 1-2 cans salmon
- 1 jar marinara sauce
- ¼ cup parsley (chopped)

Preparation:
1. Boil the pasta and heat the marinara sauce.
2. Meanwhile, heat a pan with olive oil. Sauté the garlic until lightly browned. Add the anchovies and break them until they dissolve. Roughly chop the capers and add them to the pan. Continue with the chilli flakes.

3. Place the cooked pasta in the pan. Toss to coat well. Then gradually add the marinara until all the noodles are finely coated with the sauce.
4. Pour 1-2 cans of salmon over the pasta, including the oil. Mix gently to distribute the salmon without breaking the pieces too much.
5. Garnish with fresh parsley and serve!

Serving Suggestion: Serve the Salmon tomato pasta with salad.

Variation Tip: Use angel hair or any kind of pasta.

Nutritional Information Per Serving:
Calories 438 | Fat 11g |Sodium 915mg | Carbs 64g | Fiber 4g | Sugar 6g | Protein 21g

Honey Shrimp with Pecans

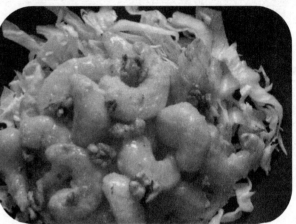

Prep Time: 15 minutes.
Cook Time: 15 minutes.
Serves: 2
Ingredients:
- ½ cup water
- ⅓ cup white sugar
- ¼ cup pecans
- 2 egg whites
- ⅓ cup mochiko
- ⅛ cup mayonnaise
- ½ pound large shrimp, peeled and deveined
- 1 tablespoon honey
- ½ tablespoon almond milk
- ½ cup vegetable oil for frying

Preparation:
1. Combine the water and sugar in a small saucepan. Bring to a boil and add the pecans. Bake for 2 minutes, then drain and place the nuts on a baking sheet to dry.
2. In a medium bowl, beat the egg whites until frothy. Add the mochiko until it has a pasty consistency. Heat the oil in a deep skillet over medium heat. Dip the shrimp in the mochiko paste then brown them in hot oil for approximately, remove them with a skimmer and drain them on paper towels.
3. In a medium bowl, combine mayonnaise, honey and almond milk. Add the shrimp and toss to coat them with the sauce. Spread the candied nuts on top and serve.

Serving Suggestion: Serve the Honey Shrimp with Pecans with rice.

Variation Tip: Use walnuts.

Nutritional Information Per Serving:
Calories 562 | Fat 2.2g |Sodium 288mg | Carbs 73.2g | Fiber 1.1g | Sugar 45.9g | Protein 39.9g

Spicy Szechuan Peppercorn Salmon

Prep Time: 15 minutes.
Cook Time: 10minutes.
Serves: 4
Ingredients:
- 2 teaspoons Szechuan peppercorns
- 4 cloves garlic, coarsely chopped
- ½ teaspoon grated lime zest
- ½ teaspoon coarse salt
- 1 (6 ounce) fillets salmon
- ½ teaspoon olive oil
- ½ tablespoon soy sauce

Preparation:
1. Preheat the grill in the oven and place the oven rack about 15 cm from the heat source. Cover a baking sheet with foil.
2. Using a mortar or spice grinder, crush the peppercorns, chopped garlic, lime zest, and salt until the peppercorns are finely ground. Rub the salmon fillets with olive oil, then place them skin side down in the prepared pan. Rub the salmon fillets with the spice mixture.
3. Grill, 10 to 15 minutes, until the salmon is flaky and no longer pink in the middle. Drizzle with soy sauce and serve.

Serving Suggestion: Serve the Szechuan Peppercorn Salmon with rice.
Variation Tip: Use tuna.
Nutritional Information Per Serving:
Calories 301 | Fat 14.1g |Sodium 768mg | Carbs 1.6 g | Fiber 0.2g | Sugar 0.2g | Protein 41.9g

Stir-fried Shrimp with Mushrooms

Prep Time: 20 minutes.
Cook Time: 10 minutes.
Serves: 2
Ingredients:
- ½ tablespoon sesame oil
- ½ tablespoon olive oil
- ½ pound tiger shrimp, peeled and deveined
- ½ cup chopped onion
- ¾ cup sliced king mushrooms
- ¼ cup chopped green bell pepper
- 2 cloves garlic, finely chopped
- ½ teaspoon minced fresh ginger
- ¼ cup water
- ½ teaspoon oyster sauce, or to taste
- ½ pound fresh Chinese wheat noodles
- 1 cup bean sprout

Preparation:
1. Heat the sesame oil and olive oil in a large wok or skillet over medium heat; Cook and toss the shrimp and onions in hot oil until covered. Combine mushrooms, green peppers and garlic into the shrimp mixture, stirring constantly. Add the ginger and stir.
2. Pour water and oyster sauce over shrimp mixture; Simmer until the shrimp are light pink on the outside and the flesh in the center is no longer translucent, 5 minutes. Mix well.
3. Toss noodles and bean sprouts with shrimp mixture; stir to combine. Cook until noodles are heated through, 2 minutes. Mix again.

Serving Suggestion: Serve the Stir-fried Shrimp with Mushrooms with noodles.
Variation Tip: Use rice noodles.
Nutritional Information Per Serving:
Calories 381 | Fat 11.1g |Sodium 495mg | Carbs 38.1g | Fiber 2.3g | Sugar 2.5g | Protein 33.9g

Crispy Shrimp Cakes

Prep Time: 30 minutes.
Cook Time: 15 minutes.
Serves: 4
Ingredients:
- 1-pound shrimp
- 1 small carrot (about 50g)
- 5 water chestnuts
- ¼ cup cilantro
- 1 teaspoon ginger (grated)
- 2 teaspoons Shaoxing wine
- ½ teaspoon salt
- ⅛ teaspoon ground white pepper
- 2 teaspoons oyster sauce
- 1 teaspoon sesame oil
- ¼ teaspoon sugar
- 1 teaspoon corn-starch
- 1 egg white
- 3 tablespoons oil

Preparation:
1. Pat the shrimp dry with a paper towel. "Crush" lightly with the side of a knife and roughly chop. Be careful not to chop the shrimp that are too small.

2. Cut a small carrot (approx. 50 g) crosswise then lengthwise and blanch the pieces in boiling water for about 2 minutes until slightly tender. Drain and finely chop the pruned carrot.

3. In a bowl, coarsely chopped shrimp, finely chopped carrots, chopped water chestnuts, ¼ cup cilantro, 1 teaspoon of grated ginger, 2 teaspoons of Shaoxing wine, ½ teaspoon of salt, ⅛ teaspoon of ground white pepper, mix 2 teaspoons of oyster sauce, 1 teaspoon of sesame oil, ¼ teaspoon of sugar, 1 teaspoon of corn-starch and 1 egg white. Beat everything for about 5 to 10 minutes one way, until the mixture is sticky and all the ingredients are well combined. It should fit into a big smooth ball with a rubber spatula. It should be sticky and cohesive.

4. Now heat a flat-bottomed pan over medium heat (non-stick or cast iron works best) until it starts to smoke lightly. Add 2 tablespoons of oil and reduce the heat to medium. Take a large tablespoon of the shrimp mixture and use another spoon to form a ball. You can also do this with oiled hands.

5. Place it in the pan and quickly squeeze it into a slice. (To avoid sticking, you can coat the spoons with oil beforehand.)

6. Fry for about 3 minutes on each side, until golden brown. Add the last tablespoon of oil during the pan if necessary.

Serving Suggestion: Serve the Shrimp cakes with ketchup.

Variation Tip: Use broccoli.

Nutritional Information Per Serving:
Calories 188 | Fat 10g |Sodium 408mg | Carbs 3g | Fiber 1g | Sugar 1g | Protein 19g

Steamed Ginger Fish

Prep Time: 15 minutes.
Cook Time: 10 to 12 minutes.
Serves:4
Ingredients:
• 2-pound halibut fillet
• 2 teaspoons coarse sea salt or kosher salt
• 2 tablespoons minced fresh ginger
• 6 tablespoons thinly sliced green onion
• 2 tablespoons dark soy sauce
• 2 tablespoons light soy sauce

• 2 tablespoons peanut oil
• 4 teaspoons toasted sesame oil
• ½ cup lightly packed fresh cilantro sprigs

Preparation:
1. Pat the halibut dry with paper towels. Rub both sides of the steak with salt. Spread the ginger over the fish and place it on a heat-resistant ceramic plate.

2. Gently put boiling water in a bamboo steamer for several inches and cover. Gently steam for 10 to 12 minutes.

3. Pour the accumulated water into the plate and sprinkle the fillet with green onions. Pour the two soy sauces over the surface of the fish.

4. In a small skillet, heat the peanut and sesame oils over medium heat until they begin to smoke. When the oil is hot, gently pour over the halibut fillet. Very hot oil will pop the spring onions and water on the fish and splash all over; pay attention. Decorate with sprigs of coriander and serve immediately.

Serving Suggestion: Serve the Steamed Fish with Ginger with rice.

Variation Tip: Use any kind of fish like tuna, salmon.

Nutritional Information Per Serving:
Calories 328 | Fat 14.8g |Sodium 6640mg | Carbs 22.7g | Fiber 0.6g | Sugar 17.9g | Protein 32.9g

Shrimp and Steamed Broccoli in Garlic Sauce

Prep Time: 15 minutes.
Cook Time: 15 minutes.
Serves:2
Ingredients:
• 1 cup fresh broccoli florets
• ½ tablespoon water
• 1 tablespoon peanut oil
• 2 large cloves garlic, minced
• ½ cup low-sodium chicken broth
• ½ tablespoon soy sauce
• ½ tablespoon oyster sauce
• 1 teaspoon grated fresh ginger root
• ½ pound uncooked medium shrimp, peeled and deveined
• ⅛ cup canned water chestnuts, drained
• 1 tablespoon corn-starch

Preparation:
1. Combine broccoli and water in a glass bowl; Microwave until slightly soft, 2 to 3 minutes.

2. Heat the peanut oil in a large skillet or wok over medium heat. Cook the garlic in hot oil until fragrant, about 1 minute.

3. Reduce the heat to a minimum; Add the chicken broth, soy sauce, oyster sauce and garlic-ginger root. Bring the mixture to a boil and add the shrimp; cook, stirring constantly, until shrimp turn pink, 3 to 4 minutes.

4. Toss the steamed broccoli and water chestnuts with the shrimp mixture to pour over the sauce. Add 1 tablespoon of corn-starch to the mixture at a time until the sauce thickens, about 5 minutes.
Serving Suggestion: Serve the Shrimp and Steamed Broccoli in Garlic Sauce with rice or noodles.
Variation Tip: Use hazelnuts if not getting chestnut.
Nutritional Information Per Serving:
Calories 213 | Fat 8.3g |Sodium 543mg | Carbs 9.1g | Fiber 1.3g | Sugar 0.9g | Protein 26.9g

Tender Shrimp with Lobster Sauce

Prep Time: 15 minutes.
Cook Time: 15 minutes.
Serves:8
Ingredients:
• 3 teaspoons corn-starch
• 4 teaspoons cooking sherry
• 2-pound medium shrimp, peeled and deveined
• 8 tablespoons vegetable oil
• 4 cloves garlic, minced
• ½ pound ground pork
• 2 cups water
• 4 tablespoons soy sauce
• ½ teaspoon sugar
• 1 teaspoon salt
• 3 tablespoons corn-starch
• ½ cup cold water
• 2 eggs, beaten
Preparation:
1. Dissolve 3 teaspoons of corn-starch in sherry in a medium bowl. Place the shrimp in the bowl and toss to coat.
2. Heat the oil in a wok or large skillet over medium heat. Add the shrimps and cook for 3 to 5 minutes in pink. Place the shrimp on a plate with a skimmer and leave as much oil as possible in the pan. Put the garlic in the hot oil and sauté for a few seconds, then add the ground pork. Cook, stirring constantly, until the pork is no longer pink.
3. Combine 1 cup of water, soy sauce, sugar and salt; Incorporate the wok with the pork. Bring to a boil, cover, reduce heat to medium and simmer for about 2 minutes. Combine the remaining 3 tablespoons of corn-starch and ½ cup of cold water.
4. Add the pork to the pan and add the shrimp to the pan as well. Bring back to a boil and stir quickly, basting the beaten egg. Serve hot over rice.
Serving Suggestion: Serve the Tender Shrimp with Lobster Sauce with rice.
Variation Tip: Use ground beef or chicken.
Nutritional Information Per Serving:
Calories 309 | Fat 16.1g |Sodium 1032mg | Carbs 6.9g | Fiber 0.1g | Sugar 0.5g | Protein 33.7g

Garlicky Pan-Fried Cod

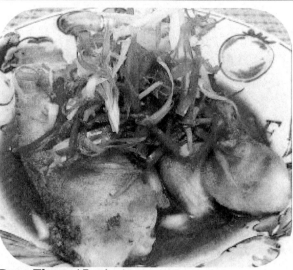

Prep Time: 15 minutes
Cook Time: 16 minutes
Servings: 2
Ingredients:
For cod:
• 8½ ounces cod fillet
• Pinch of salt and freshly ground black pepper
• 2-3 tablespoons corn-starch
• 2 tablespoons vegetable oil
• 2 scallions, sliced
• 1 (1-inch) piece fresh ginger, sliced thinly
• 4 garlic cloves, chopped
• ½ of red chili, sliced
For sauce:
• ¼ cup water
• 1 tablespoon light soy sauce
• 2 teaspoons sugar
Preparation:
1. Season the cod fillet with a pinch of salt and black pepper.
2. Dust the cod fillet with corn-starch evenly.
3. Then shake the fillet to remove excess starch. Set aside.
4. For sauce: in a bowl, add all ingredients and mix until well combined. Set aside.
5. In a frying pan, heat the oil over high heat and sauté the scallions, ginger, garlic and red chili for about 1-2 minutes.
6. With a slotted spoon, transfer the scallion mixture onto a plate. Set aside.
7. In the same pan, add the cod fillet and cook for about 5 minutes per side.
8. With a slotted spoon, transfer the cod fillet onto a serving plate.
9. In the same pan, add the sauce over medium heat and cook for about 2-3 minutes.
10. Stir in the cooked scallion mixture and cook for about 1 minute.
11. Pour the sauce onto the fish and serve immediately.
Serving Suggestions: Serve with fresh veggie salad.
Variation Tip: You can also use all-purpose flour to dust the fish instead of corn-starch.
Nutritional Information per Serving:
Calories: 290 | Fat: 14.9g|Sat Fat: 2.7g|Carbohydrates: 16.9g|Fiber: 1g|Sugar: 4.6g|Protein: 22.9g

Aromatic Lemon Fish with Sesame Seeds

Prep Time: 15 minutes
Cook Time: 13 minutes
Servings: 8
Ingredients:
For fish:
- 1 egg white
- 2 tablespoons soy sauce
- 1 tablespoon Chinese Shaoxing wine
- 2 pounds white fish fillets, cut into bite-sized pieces
- 1 cup all-purpose flour
- 2-3 cups vegetable oil
- 2-3 scallions, chopped
- 1 teaspoon sesame seeds

For sauce:
- 4 tablespoons sugar
- ¼ cup chicken broth
- 1 tablespoon soy sauce
- 1 tablespoon vegetable oil
- 1 small garlic clove, grated finely
- 2 tablespoons fresh lemon juice
- ½ teaspoon lemon zest, grated finely
- 2 teaspoons corn-starch
- 2 tablespoons water

Preparation:
1. For fish: in a bowl, add the egg white, soy sauce and wine and mix well.
2. Add the fish pieces and coat with the mixture evenly. Set aside for about 10-15 minutes.
3. For sauce: in a bowl, add the sugar, broth and soy sauce and beat until well combined.
4. In another small bowl, dissolve the corn-starch in water.
5. In a small pan, heat the oil over medium heat and sauté the garlic for about 10 seconds.
6. Stir in the broth mixture and cook for about 2-3 minutes, stirring continuously.
7. Stir in the lemon juice and zest and cook for about 30 seconds.
8. Add the corn-starch mixture and cook for about 30 seconds, stirring continuously.
9. Remove from the heat and set aside to cool.
10. Coat the marinated fish pieces with flour evenly.
11. In a deep skillet, heat the vegetable oil over high heat and fry the fish pieces in 2 batches for about 3-4 minutes or until cooked through.
12. With a slotted spoon, transfer the fish pieces onto a paper towels-lined plate to drain.
13. Now transfer the fish pieces onto a serving platter and top with sauce.

14. Garnish with scallion and sesame seeds and serve immediately.
Serving Suggestions: Serve with the garnishing of lemon slices.
Variation Tip: You could use apple juice instead of the Shaoxing wine.
Nutritional Information per Serving:
Calories: 772 | Fat: 63.5g|Sat Fat: 12.1g|Carbohydrates: 19.7g|Fiber: 0.7g|Sugar: 6.4g|Protein: 30.5g

Sweet & Sour Cod with Pineapple

Prep Time: 20 minutes
Cook Time: 10 minutes
Servings: 4
Ingredients:
For fish:
- ¾ cup all-purpose flour
- 1 tablespoon corn-starch
- ¼ teaspoon baking powder
- ⅛ teaspoon ground turmeric
- Salt and freshly ground white pepper, to taste
- ⅔ cup cold club soda
- ¼ teaspoon sesame oil
- 12 ounces cod fillet, cut into 1-inch cubes
- 1-2 cups canola oil

For Sauce:
- ¾ cup canned pineapple chunks
- ¾ cup canned pineapple juice
- 2½ tablespoons red wine vinegar
- ⅓ cup plus 2 tablespoons water, divided
- 2 tablespoons sugar
- ¼ teaspoon salt
- 1½ tablespoons corn-starch
- ¼ cup green bell peppers, seeded and cut into 1-inch cubes
- ¼ cup red bell peppers, seeded and cut into 1-inch cubes
- ¼ cup red onion, cut into 1-inch cubes
- 1 tablespoon ketchup

Preparation:
1. In a bowl, add flour, corn-starch, baking powder, corn-starch, turmeric, salt and white pepper and mix well.
2. Add the club soda and sesame oil and mix until smooth.
3. Coat the fish cubes with mixture evenly.
4. In a deep skillet, heat canola oil over medium heat and fry the fish cubes in 2 batches for about 3-4 minutes or until golden brown.
5. With a slotted spoon, transfer the fish cubes onto a paper towels-lined plate to drain.

6. Meanwhile, for sauce: in a bowl, add the pineapple, pineapple juice, vinegar, ⅓ cup of water, sugar and salt and mix well. Set aside.

7. In a small bowl, dissolve the corn-starch into the remaining water. Set aside.

8. In a large non-stick skillet, add 2 teaspoons of the frying oil over high heat and stir fry the bell peppers and onion for about 1-1½ minutes.

9. Stir in the ketchup and stir fry for about 20-30 seconds.

10. Stir in the pineapple mixture and cook for about 2 minutes.

11. Slowly add the corn-starch mixture, stirring continuously.

12. Cook for about 1-2 minutes, stirring continuously.

13. Add the cooked fish cubes and gently stir to combine.

14. Serve immediately.

Serving Suggestions: Serve with cooked rice.
Variation Tip: You can substitute club soda with tonic water.
Nutritional Information per Serving:
Calories: 733 | Fat: 55.4g|Sat Fat: 4.1g|Carbohydrates: 41.6g|Fiber: 1.6g|Sugar: 15.7g|Protein: 18.3g

Honey Shrimp and Walnuts

Prep Time: 15 minutes
Cook Time: 15 minutes
Servings: 4
Ingredients:
• 1 cup water
• ⅔ cup white sugar
• ½ cup walnuts
• 4 egg whites
• ⅔ cup glutinous rice flour
• 1 pound large shrimp, peeled and deveined
• ¼ cup mayonnaise
• 2 tablespoons honey
• 1 tablespoon sweetened condensed milk
• 1 cup vegetable oil
• 2 tablespoons scallion greens, chopped
Preparation:
1. In a small pan, add the water and sugar over medium heat and bring to a boil.
2. Stir in the walnuts and cook for about 2 minutes.
3. Remove from the heat and drain the walnuts.
4. Arrange the walnuts onto a baking sheet in a single layer and set aside to dry.
5. In a bowl, add egg whites and eat until foamy.
6. Add the rice flour and stir until smooth.
7. Coat the shrimp with rice flour mixture evenly.
8. In a heavy deep skillet, heat the oil over medium-high heat and fry the shrimp in 2 batches for about 5 minutes or until golden brown.

9. With a slotted spoon, transfer the shrimp onto a paper towels-lined plate to drain.

10. In a serving bowl, add the mayonnaise, honey and condensed milk and mix well.

11. Add the cooked shrimp and toss to coat well.

12. Sprinkle with candied walnuts and scallion greens and serve.

Serving Suggestions: Serve with fresh salad.
Variation Tip: You can cut off the ratio of sugar according to your taste.
Nutritional Information per Serving:
Calories: 980 | Fat: 60.4g|Sat Fat: 9g|Carbohydrates: 72.4g|Fiber: 1.7g|Sugar: 45.9g|Protein: 35.3g

Flavorful Shrimp in Sweet & Sour Sauce

Prep Time: 15 minutes
Cook Time: 10 minutes
Servings: 2
Ingredients:
For sauce:
• 3 tablespoons fresh orange juice
• 1 tablespoon honey
• 1 tablespoon low-sodium soy sauce
• ½ tablespoon balsamic vinegar
For shrimp:
• ¾ pound shrimp, peeled and deveined
• ½ tablespoon arrowroot powder
• 1 tablespoon canola oil
• 2 garlic cloves, minced
• 1 teaspoon fresh ginger, minced
Preparation:
1. For sauce: in a bowl, add all ingredients and mix well. Set aside.
2. In a bowl, add shrimp and arrowroot powder and toss to coat well.
3. In a large skillet, heat oil over medium-high heat and sauté the garlic and ginger for about 1 minute.
4. Add shrimp and cook for about 2 minutes.
5. Add sauce and cook for about 2 minutes, stirring continuously.
6. With a slotted spoon, transfer the shrimp into a bowl.
7. Cook for about 2-4 minutes or until desired thickness, stirring continuously.
8. Serve shrimp with the topping of sauce.
Serving Suggestions: Serve with orange slices.
Variation Tip: Use raw shrimp for this recipe.
Nutritional Information per Serving:
Calories: 217 | Fat: 6.7g|Sat Fat: 1g|Carbohydrates: 11.8g|Fiber: 0.2g|Sugar: 7.4g|Protein: 26.5g

Sichuan Prawns Stir Fry

Prep Time: 15 minutes
Cook Time: 6 minutes
Servings: 3
Ingredients:
- 1½ tablespoons groundnut oil
- 1 scallion, chopped finely
- 1 tablespoon fresh ginger, chopped finely
- 2 garlic cloves, minced
- 1-pound raw prawns, peeled and deveined
- 1 tablespoon tomato puree
- 3 teaspoons chili bean sauce
- 2 teaspoons Chinese black vinegar
- 2 teaspoons sesame oil
- 1 teaspoon cider vinegar
- 2 teaspoons golden caster sugar
- ½ teaspoon salt
- ½ teaspoon freshly ground black pepper
- 2 tablespoons scallion greens, sliced

Preparation:
1. In a large skillet, heat oil over medium heat and stir fry scallion, ginger and garlic for about 1 minute.
2. Add prawns and stir fry for about 1 minute.
3. Add remaining ingredients except for scallion greens and stir fry for about 3-4 minutes.
4. Serve hot with the garnishing of scallion greens.
Serving Suggestions: Serve with fresh lime slices.
Variation Tip: Avoid prawns that smell like ammonia.
Nutritional Information per Serving:
Calories: 325 | Fat: 14.2g|Sat Fat: 2.4g|Carbohydrates: 12g|Fiber: 0.6g|Sugar: 6.1g|Protein: 36g

Chinese Steamed Whole Sea Bass

Prep Time: 15 minutes
Cook Time: 10 minutes
Servings: 3
Ingredients:
- 1-pound whole sea bass, cleaned, rinsed and patted dry
- Salt, to taste
- ¼ cup fresh ginger, sliced thinly

- 5 scallions, sliced thinly
- ¼ cup chili oil
- ¼ cup soy sauce
- 1 tablespoon white sugar
- 2 tablespoons fresh cilantro leaves
- 1 small red chili, sliced

Preparation:
1. Season the sea bass with salt evenly.
2. In a large ceramic plate, place about ⅓ of the ginger slices and 2 scallions and then arrange sea bass on top.
3. Spread the remaining ginger slices and scallions over the sea bass evenly.
4. In a large pan of boiling water, arrange a rack.
5. Place the plate of sea bass over the rack and steam, covered for about 8-10 minutes.
6. Remove from the pan and discard any liquid from the plate.
7. In a bowl, add the chili oil, soy sauce and sugar and mix until sugar is dissolved.
8. Place the sauce over the sea bass and serve with the garnishing of cilantro and red chili.
Serving Suggestions: Grilled veggies will go great with this fish.
Variation Tip: Remember to trim off the fins from fish before cooking.
Nutritional Information per Serving:
Calories: 481 | Fat: 33.1g|Sat Fat: 5.8g|Carbohydrates: 12.7g|Fiber: 2.5g|Sugar: 5.3g|Protein: 36g

Steamed Halibut with Scallion

Prep Time: 15 minutes
Cook Time: 12 minutes
Servings: 4
Ingredients:
For sauce:
- 3 tablespoons canola oil
- 1 tablespoon dark soy sauce
- 1 tablespoon light soy sauce
- 1 teaspoon oyster sauce
- 1 teaspoon sesame oil, toasted
- 2 tablespoons fresh ginger, slivered
- 2 garlic cloves, minced
- ½ teaspoon corn-starch
- ½ teaspoon granulated sugar
- ⅛ teaspoon freshly ground white pepper
For fish:
- 4 (6-ounce) halibut fillets
- 2 tablespoons canola oil
- ¼ cup scallion, sliced
Preparation:

1. For sauce: in a bowl, add all ingredients and beat until well combined. Set aside.
2. In a large ceramic plate, place the halibut fillets in a single layer and top with some of the sauce.
3. Spread the remaining ginger slices and scallions over the sea bass evenly.
4. In a large pan of boiling water, arrange a rack.
5. Place the plate of sea bass over the rack and steam, covered for about 7-10 minutes.
6. Remove from the heat and transfer the fillets onto a serving platter and top with the remaining sauce and scallion slices.
7. In a small frying pan, heat the oil until smoking.
8. Pour the hot oil over fillets and serve immediately.
Serving Suggestions: Serve with poattao wedges.
Variation Tip: If you don't have a steamer plate, then steam the fish in a steamer basket, arranged over a pan of boiling water.
Nutritional Information per Serving:
Calories: 373 | Fat: 22.8g|Sat Fat: 2g|Carbohydrates: 3.8g|Fiber: 0.6g|Sugar: 0.9g|Protein: 36.5g

Crispy Shrimp Toast

Prep Time: 20 minutes
Cook Time: 38 minutes
Servings: 10
Ingredients:
• 5 white bread slices, crust removed and cut into 4 triangles diagonally
• ½ pound raw shrimp, peeled and deveined
• 2 teaspoons lard
• 4 water chestnuts, chopped finely
• ½ tomato, chopped finely
• 2 scallions, chopped finely
• 1 teaspoon fresh ginger, grated
• 1 teaspoon Chinese rice wine
• 1 large egg, beaten lightly
• 2 teaspoons corn-starch
• Salt and freshly ground black pepper, or to taste
• 2 cups canola oil
Preparation:
1. Preheat the oven to 225 degrees F.
2. Arrange the bread slices onto a 9x13-inch non-stick baking sheet in a single layer.
3. Bake for about 30 minutes.
4. Meanwhile, in a food processor with a knife blade, add the shrimp and lard and pulse until chopped finely.
5. Add the water chestnuts, tomato, scallion and ginger and pulse until combined.
6. Add the remaining ingredients except the oil and pulse smooth.
7. Spread about 2 teaspoons of the shrimp paste over each toasted bread slice evenly.

8. In a deep skillet, heat the oil to 350 degrees F and deep fry the toasts in 3-4 batches for about 1½ minutes.
9. Flip and cook for about 15 seconds.
10. With a slotted spoon, transfer the toasts onto a paper towel-lined plate to drain.
11. Serve warm.
Serving Suggestions: Serve with chili sauce.
Variation Tip: Don't forget to remove the crust from bread slices.
Nutritional Information per Serving:
Calories: 439 | Fat: 41.7g|Sat Fat: 3.6g|Carbohydrates: 10.8g|Fiber: 0.4g|Sugar: 0.8g|Protein: 6.5g

Chinese Crab Rangoon

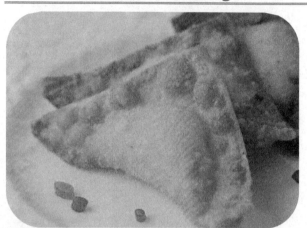

Prep Time: 20 minutes
Cook Time: 16 minutes
Servings: 20
Ingredients:
• ½ pound lump crab meat
• 1 (8-ounce) package cream cheese, softened
• 3 scallions, chopped finely
• 1 teaspoon low-sodium soy sauce
• 1 teaspoon Worcestershire sauce
• 1 teaspoon sugar
• 20 wonton wrappers
• 2-3 cups vegetable oil
Preparation:
1. For filling: in a large bowl, add all the ingredients except the wrappers sand mix until smooth.
2. Arrange 1 wonton wrapper onto a smooth surface.
3. Place 1 teaspoonful of filling in the center of the wrapper and with wet fingers, moisten the edges.
4. Fold the wrapper in half to form a triangle and press the edges to seal.
5. Repeat with the remaining wrappers and filling.
6. In a deep skillet, heat the oil over medium heat and deep fry the wontons in 3-4 batches for about 1-2 minutes per side or until golden crispy.
7. With a slotted spoon, transfer the wontons onto a paper towel-lined plate to drain completely.
8. Serve warm.
Serving Suggestions: Serve with a dipping sauce of choice.
Variation Tip: The temperature of frying oil should be in the 350-375 degrees F range.
Nutritional Information per Serving:
Calories: 336 | Fat: 27.1g|Sat Fat: 6.9g|Carbohydrates: 19.5g|Fiber: 0.6g|Sugar: 0.3g|Protein: 5.7g

Fish Tofu Soup with Mushrooms

Prep Time: 20 minutes.
Cook Time: 15 minutes.
Serves:4
Ingredients:
For the fish & marinade:
• 8 ounces tuna fillet
• ½ teaspoon corn-starch
• 1 teaspoon light soy sauce
• 1 teaspoon Shaoxing wine
• ¼ teaspoon sesame oil
• ¼ teaspoon salt
• ⅛ teaspoon white pepper
For the soup:
• 2 tablespoons oil
• 1-2 thinly sliced ginger
• 6 fresh shiitake mushrooms
• 6 dried red chilies
• 1 cup soybean sprouts
• 4 cups chicken stock
• 1 ½ cups water
• 1 cup cabbage (cut into 1-inch pieces)
• ½ pound firm tofu
• ½ teaspoon sesame oil
• Salt (to taste)
• Chopped scallion
• Chopped cilantro
Preparation:
1. Start by marinating the tuna. Combine the fish ingredients and marinade in a bowl and set aside while you cook the other ingredients (about 15-20 minutes). You should have all the ingredients ready before you turn on the stove!
2. When you are ready to cook, heat 2 tablespoons of oil in a large wok over medium heat. Add the ginger and mushrooms and sauté for 2 minutes until fragrant and lightly golden. Add the dried peppers, if used, and cook for another 30 seconds. Add the bean sprouts and stir for another minute.
3. Add the chicken broth, water, cabbage, sliced tofu and sesame oil. Bring to a boil and season with salt.
4. Once it boils, place each piece of fish on top of the soup (do this one at a time. You don't want the fish to stick together in a bundle). The fire should still be medium to high. Gently move the fish around the soup so that each piece is submerged in the hot liquid. Bring the soup to a boil and you're done. Serve with chives and cilantro.
Serving Suggestion: Serve the Fish Tofu Soup with noodles.
Variation Tip: Use any kind of fish.
Nutritional Information Per Serving:
Calories 234| Fat 11g |Sodium 634mg | Carbs 9g | Fiber 1g | Sugar 2g | Protein 23g

Chicken Mushroom Soup with Dates

Prep Time: 05 minutes.
Cook Time: 1 hour 15 minutes.
Serves:8
Ingredients:
• 20 small dried shiitake mushrooms
• 8 cups water
• 2 tablespoons dried goji berries
• 4 dried Chinese dates
• 1 small organic chicken
• 1 tablespoon oil
• 5 slices ginger
• 2 tablespoons Shaoxing wine
• Salt (to taste)
• 1 scallion, finely chopped
Preparation:
1. First wash the dried shiitake mushrooms several times and rinse well. Then soak in 8 cups of water in the pot for 6 hours or overnight. Cut the stems (after soaking) before cooking and return the mushrooms to the pot of water.
2. Add dried goji berries and dried Chinese dates to the pot (without soaking first). Bring to a boil over high heat, then immediately reduce the heat to low.
3. Prepare the chicken while you let it simmer. Wash the chicken and pat it dry with a paper towel. Cut the chicken breast and set it aside for another dish. Cut the rest of the chicken into large pieces. Put aside.
4. After the soup has simmered for 30 minutes, heat a wok over medium heat until it begins to smoke lightly. Reduce the heat to medium and add the oil and the ginger slices. Cook for a minute or two.
5. Spread the oil around the wok to coat it. Then spread the chicken in a single layer and lightly brown the chicken before stirring. After most of each piece is cooked, turn off the heat.
6. Place the chicken in the pot. Deglaze the wok with ½ cup of water and also add to the pot. Finally add the Shaoxing wine and cover. Cook over low heat for another 30 minutes over medium heat. Salt and sprinkle with chopped chives just before serving.
Serving Suggestion: Serve the Chicken mushroom soup with noodles or salad.
Variation Tip: Use gooseberries.
Nutritional Information Per Serving:
Calories 273 | Fat 16.1g |Sodium 380mg | Carbs 5g | Fiber 1g | Sugar 2g | Protein 21g

Chinese Rice Cake and Veggies Soup

Prep Time: 25 minutes.
Cook Time: 20 minutes.
Serves: 4
Ingredients:
For the meat & marinade:
• 4 ounces lean pork (cut into small, thin strips)
• 1 teaspoon Shaoxing wine
• ½ tablespoon light soy sauce
• ¼ teaspoon sesame oil
• ⅛ teaspoon white pepper
• 1 teaspoons corn-starch
• ½ teaspoon water
To assemble the soup:
• 2 tablespoons vegetable oil(divided)
• 2 slices ginger (julienned)
• 2 scallions (thinly sliced on an angle, white and green parts separated)
• ½ small carrot (thinly sliced)
• 1 pound cabbage (stems cut into ½-inch pieces and leaves cut into 1-inch pieces)
• 2 cups low sodium chicken stock
• 2 cups water
• ¼ teaspoon white pepper
• ½ teaspoon sesame oil
• ½ tablespoon light soy sauce
• ½ pound rice cakes
Preparation:
1. Toss the pork (or chicken) with the Shaoxing wine, light soy sauce, sesame oil, white pepper, corn-starch and water. Marinate 15 to 20 minutes.
2. Preheat your wok until it begins to smoke lightly. Add 2 tablespoons of oil over high heat and brown the pork until golden brown. Remove the pork from the wok and set it aside.
3. Reduce the heat to medium and add an additional 2 tablespoons of oil to the wok along with the ginger and the white pieces of chives. Cook for 1 minute and add the carrots. Cook for another minute and add the cabbage. Fry everything for a few minutes until the Napa cabbage leaves are tender.
4. Add 4 cups of low sodium chicken broth and 4 cups of water. Bring everything to a boil, then lower the heat and simmer for 5 minutes, until the thick stems of the cabbage are tender.
5. Add salt, ½ teaspoon of white pepper, 1 teaspoon of sesame oil and 1 tablespoon of light soy sauce to taste.
6. Add the cooked pork and sprinkle the rice cakes over the soup with the green chives. The rice cakes should rest on the soup so that they do not sink in and stick to the bottom of the wok / pot. Cover and cook for another minute or until rice cakes are done (see recipe notes if using dry rice cakes). Salt again and serve!
Serving Suggestion: Serve the Chinese rice cake soup with noodles.

Variation Tip: Use chicken.
Nutritional Information Per Serving:
Calories 368| Fat 14g |Sodium 482mg | Carbs 46g | Fiber 1g | Sugar 2g | Protein 17g

Melon and Glass Noodles Soup with Meatballs

Prep Time: 45 minutes.
Cook Time: 30 minutes.
Serves: 8
Ingredients:
For the meatballs:
• 1 pound ground pork
• 2 tablespoons water
• 2 ½ tablespoons light soy sauce
• 2 tablespoons Shaoxing wine
• 1 teaspoon sesame oil
• ½ teaspoon ground white pepper
• ½ teaspoon sugar
• 1 egg white
• 1 tablespoon ginger (minced)
• 1 scallion (finely chopped)
• ¼ teaspoon salt
For the rest of the soup:
• 1 package glass noodles
• 1 pound winter melon (450g)
• 1 tablespoon oil
• 2 scallions only white part
• 4 cups chicken stock
• 2 cups water
• ½ teaspoon ground white pepper
• ½ teaspoon sesame oil
• salt (to taste)
• large handful of cilantro
Preparation:
To make the balls:
1. Put all the ingredients for the meatballs in a large bowl and beat by hand with a pair of toothpicks one way for at least 10 minutes. Use a vigorous circular motion until the ground pork mixture becomes thick and mushy, with some resistance when beating. It's actually best done by hand, but you can use the paddle attachment on your electric mixer on low speed for 6-7 minutes for a similar effect.
2. Now form the meatballs. Brush both palms of your hands with oil to prevent sticking, take a large tablespoon of the meat mixture and roll it into a ball with both palms. The meatballs should be the size of a golf ball. Place them on a lightly greased baking sheet with a space between them. Cool while you prepare the rest of the soup.
To assemble the soup:
3. Soak the glass noodles in cold water for 15 minutes. Drain the noodles and cut it in half lengthwise. Put aside.

4. Cut the winter melon and cut off the outer ¾ inch of the dark green skin. Rinse and cut into ¼-inch-thick pieces.

5. Put a pot on medium heat and add 1 tablespoon of oil. Cook the white parts of the chives for about 1 minute. Then add 4 cups of chicken broth, 2 cups of water and the winter melon. Increase the heat and bring to a boil.

6. When the soup boils, use a spoon to gently lower the meatballs into the soup. Add ½ teaspoon of ground white pepper and ½ teaspoon of sesame oil. Return to a boil. Add the glass noodles, toss and season with salt. Cook another 3-4 minutes, garnish with cilantro and serve.

Serving Suggestion: Serve the Melon Soup with Meatballs with noodles.

Variation Tip: Use mung bean vermicelli.

Nutritional Information Per Serving:
Calories 259 | Fat 16.1g |Sodium 612mg | Carbs 16.9g | Fiber 1g | Sugar 1g | Protein 13.7g

Homemade Wonton Soup

Prep Time: 1 hour 15 minutes.
Cook Time: 20 minutes.
Serves:8
Ingredients:
• 10 ounces baby Bok choy
• 8 ounces ground pork
• 2 ½ tablespoons sesame oil (plus more for the stock)
• ⅛ teaspoon white pepper
• 1 tablespoon soy sauce
• ½ teaspoon salt
• 2 tablespoons Shaoxing wine
• 1 package wonton wrappers
• 6 cups chicken stock
• 1 spring onions (chopped)
Preparation:
1. Start by washing the vegetables well. Bring a large pot of water to a boil and blanch the vegetables for about 60-90 seconds until tender. Drain and rinse with cold water.

2. Take a good quantity of vegetables and carefully wring out as much water as possible. Chop the vegetables very finely (you can also speed up the process by putting them in the food processor). Repeat until all the vegetables are chopped.

3. In a medium bowl, add the finely chopped vegetables, ground pork, 2 ½ tablespoons of sesame oil, a pinch of white pepper, 1 tablespoon of soy sauce, ½ teaspoon of salt and 1-2 tablespoons of Shaoxing wine. Mix very well until the mixture is completely emulsified, almost like a paste.

4. It's time to roll! Fill a small bowl with water. Take a sleeve and wet the edges of the sleeve with your finger. Put a little more than a teaspoon of stuffing in the center. Fold the wrap in half and press firmly on both sides to seal it securely.

5. Hold the two bottom corners of the little rectangle you just created (the side that the fill is on) and bring the two corners together. You can use a little water to make sure they stick together.

6. At this point you can cook (boil) and taste a few wontons and adjust the seasoning of your filling to taste; You can always add a little more Shaoxing wine, soy sauce, sesame oil, salt and / or white pepper. according to your requirements.

7. When you are satisfied with the taste of the filling, continue to assemble until all of the filling is used up. Place the wontons on a baking sheet or plate lined with parchment paper, making sure they do not touch each other (this will prevent them from sticking).

8. If you want to freeze your wontons right away, you can cover them with plastic wrap, put the baking sheet / dish in the freezer and, after freezing, place them in freezer bags. They last a few months in the freezer and are always ready for wonton soup.

9. To make the soup, heat your chicken broth over low heat and add 2-3 teaspoons of sesame oil and white pepper and salt to taste.

10. Bring another pot of water to a boil. Gently add the wontons to the pot, one at a time. Pick up the pot and use a twisting and rotating motion to keep the pot moving and prevent the wontons from sticking to the bottom. If they stick, don't worry, they should come out freely after cooking. Once they are swimming, cook them for another 1 to 2 minutes. Be careful not to overcook them - mushy wontons are a sin! Remove the wonton with a skimmer and place it in bowls.

11. Pour the soup over the wontons and garnish with spring onions.

Serving Suggestion: Serve the Simple wonton soup with noodles.

Variation Tip: Use Swiss chard.

Nutritional Information Per Serving:
Calories 353 | Fat 16g |Sodium 889mg | Carbs 40g | Fiber 1g | Sugar 5g | Protein 17g

Oxtail Soup with Radish

Prep Time: 05 minutes.
Cook Time: 7 hours
Serves: 4
Ingredients:
• 1 ¼ pounds oxtails
• 6 cups water
• ½ large onion (cut into wedges)
• ½ medium Chinese turnip or daikon radish (cut into large chunks)
• Salt (to taste)
• chopped cilantro (to garnish)
Preparation:

1. Preheat the oven to 350 degrees Fahrenheit. Rinse the oxtails under cold water and dry them with a paper towel. Place on a baking sheet and roast for 30-40 minutes.

2. While the oxtails are frying, add 6 cups of water to a saucepan. Add the fried onions and oxtails and bring to a boil. Immediately lower the heat to a very gentle simmer. (Make sure that the heat is not too high, otherwise all the liquid will evaporate!).

3. Simmer for 6 hours (the longer the better) with the lid closed. Remember to remove the fat regularly. Add the beets about 30 minutes before serving. Cook until tender over low heat and salt the soup to taste. Serve garnished with chopped cilantro.

Serving Suggestion: Serve the Oxtail soup with noodles.

Variation Tip: Use veal.

Nutritional Information Per Serving:

Calories 366 | Fat 16.1g |Sodium 306mg | Carbs 4g | Fiber 1g | Sugar 2g | Protein 43g

Aromatic Chicken Corn Egg Drop Soup

Prep Time: 05 minutes.
Cook Time: 20 minutes.
Serves: 8
Ingredients:
- 8 ounces chicken breast
- 2 tablespoons water
- 2 teaspoons corn-starch
- 2 teaspoons oyster sauce
- 3 cups fresh or frozen sweet corn
- 10 cups chicken stock
- 1 teaspoon turmeric powder
- 1 teaspoon sesame oil
- 1 teaspoon salt (or to taste)
- 1 pinch white pepper
- ½ cup corn-starch
- 4 egg whites
- 2 green onion (chopped)
- 2 tablespoons cilantros (chopped, optional)
- Freshly ground black pepper (optional)

Preparation:
1. Marinate the chicken with 1 tablespoon of water, 1 teaspoon of corn-starch and 1 teaspoon of oyster sauce. Stir until liquid is absorbed by the chicken. Put aside.

2. Finely chop ½ cup of corn kernels and set aside. Put the chicken broth, whole and chopped corn kernels and turmeric powder in a saucepan and bring to a boil. Lower the heat, cover and simmer for 10 minutes.

3. Then add sesame oil, salt and white pepper. Turn up the heat a bit. Add the chicken to the soup and use a spoon to crush the chicken pieces while stirring for a minute.

4. Stir in the corn-starch and chicken broth again until just incorporated (as the corn-starch and water will separate if left for more than a few minutes). Use a spoon or a whisk to stir the soup and slowly pour in the corn-starch mixture. The soup will become even thicker as the corn-starch is cooked. Continue stirring for another 30 seconds. If the soup is too thick, add more broth and if it is too runny, add more corn-starch mixture until the soup is the consistency you prefer.

5. Then use a large spoon or ladle to gently stir the soup in one direction as you slowly pour the whipped egg whites into the soup. Slow agitation in a large slow circular motion creates large "ribbons" of eggs and faster agitation results in a finer "egg flower". Here, too, you can decide how you personally like the texture of the egg.

6. Add half of the chives and add the rest to serve as a garnish. If you are looking for a little more flavor, you can also drizzle sesame oil over it and sprinkle chopped cilantro and freshly ground black pepper on each bowl.

Serving Suggestion: Serve the Chicken Corn Egg Drop Soup with noodles.

Variation Tip: Use turkey.

Nutritional Information Per Serving:

Calories 182 | Fat 4g |Sodium 480mg | Carbs 24g | Fiber 1g | Sugar 5g | Protein 17g

Hot & Sour Pork and Tofu Soup

Prep Time: 20 minutes
Cook Time: 28 minutes
Servings: 4
Ingredients:
- ½ cup dried mushrooms
- 12 dried lily buds
- 3 tablespoons cold water
- 2 tablespoons corn flour
- 4 cups low-sodium chicken broth
- 2 tablespoons dark soy sauce
- 2 tablespoons white vinegar
- ½ teaspoon salt
- 2 large eggs, beaten lightly
- 1 cup spiced tofu, shredded
- ½ cup cooked pork, shredded
- ½ cup bamboo shoots, shredded
- 1½ teaspoons ground white pepper
- 1 tablespoon sesame oil
- ¼ cup scallion, chopped

Preparation:
1. In a bowl of boiling water, soak the dried mushrooms for about 25-30 minutes or until tender.

2. In another bowl of boiling water, soak the dried lily buds for about 10-15 minutes or until tender.

3. Then drain the lily buds and cut off the hard tough tips. Set aside.

4. In a small bowl, add the water and corn flour and mix until smooth. Set aside.
5. In a large soup pan, add the broth over medium heat and bring to a boil.
6. Add the soy sauce, vinegar and salt and stir to combine.
7. Slowly add the beaten eggs and cook for about 3-4 minutes, stirring continuously.
8. Add the mushrooms, lily buds, tofu, pork, bamboo shoots and white pepper and cook for about 4-5 minutes, stirring occasionally.
9. Reduce the heat to low and add in the corn flour mixture, stirring continuously.
10. Cook for about 5-8 minutes or until slightly thickened, stirring frequently.
11. Divide the soup into serving bowls and drizzle with sesame oil.
12. Serve hot with the garnishing of scallion.
Serving Suggestions: Serve with the drizzling of sesame oil.
Variation Tip: Corn flour can be replaced with cornstarch.
Nutritional Information per Serving:
Calories: 195| Fat: 9.8g|Sat Fat: 2.2g|Carbohydrates: 8g|Fiber: 1.8g|Sugar: 1.6g|Protein: 19.4g

Egg Drop Soup with Scallions

Prep Time: 10 minutes
Cook Time: 5 minutes
Servings: 2
Ingredients:
• 2 cups chicken broth
• ½ teaspoon sesame oil
• ½ teaspoon soy sauce
• 2 teaspoons corn starch
• 4 teaspoons water
• 2 eggs, beaten lightly
• Salt and ground white pepper, to taste
• 2 teaspoon scallion greens, chopped
Preparation:
1. In a pan, add the chicken broth, sesame oil and soy sauce and bring to a boil.
2. Meanwhile, in a small bowl, dissolve the corn starch in water.
3. Add the corn starch mixture into the boiling broth, stirring continuously.
4. Add the beaten eggs, stirring gently and continuously.
5. Immediately, remove from the heat and season with the salt and white pepper.
6. Serve immediately with the garnishing of scallion greens.
Serving Suggestions: Serve with crusty bread.
Variation Tip: Use good quality chicken broth.

Nutritional Information per Serving:
Calories: 124| Fat: 6.9g|Sat Fat: 1.9g|Carbohydrates: 4.5g|Fiber: 0.1g|Sugar: 1.1g|Protein: 10.5g

Fish & Tofu Soup with Veggies

Prep Time: 15 minutes
Cook Time: 10 minutes
Servings: 4
Ingredients:
For Fish Marinade:
• 1 teaspoon Shaoxing wine
• 1 teaspoon light soy sauce
• ¼ teaspoon sesame oil
• ½ teaspoon corn-starch
• ¼ teaspoon salt
• ⅛ teaspoon ground white pepper
• 8 ounces tilapia fillet, sliced thinly
For Soup:
• 2 tablespoons vegetable oil
• 6 fresh shiitake mushrooms, sliced
• 1 teaspoon fresh ginger, sliced thinly
• 1 cup soybean sprouts
• ½ pound firm tofu, pressed, drained and cubed
• 1 cup Napa cabbage, cut into 1-inch pieces
• ½ teaspoon sesame oil
• Salt, to taste
• 4 cups chicken broth
• 1½ cups water
• 2 scallions, chopped
Preparation:
1. For marinade: in a bowl, add all ingredients except for fish and mix until cornstarch is dissolved.
2. Add the fish slices and mix well.
3. Set aside for about 15-20 minutes.
4. For soup: in a large pan, heat the vegetable oil over medium heat and sauté the mushrooms and ginger for about 2 minutes.
5. Stir in the soybean sprouts and cook for about 1 minute.
6. Add the tofu, cabbage, sesame oil, salt, broth and water and bring to a boil.
7. Gently submerge the fish slices in soup and cook for about 2-4 minutes or until desired doneness.
8. Serve hot with the garnishing of scallion.
Serving Suggestions: Serve with a drizzling of lemon juice.
Variation Tip: Mung bean sprouts will also work well instead of soybean sprouts.
Nutritional Information per Serving:
Calories: 224 | Fat: 12.5g|Sat Fat: 2.6g|Carbohydrates: 6.7g|Fiber: 1.7g|Sugar: 2.4g|Protein: 23.4g

Pork & Lotus Root Soup

Prep Time: 15 minutes
Cook Time: 5 hours 6 minutes
Servings: 12
Ingredients:
- 2 pounds pork ribs
- 1 cup dried seaweed
- 1 pound lotus root, peeled and cut into chunks
- 2 tablespoons fresh ginger, sliced
- 1 tablespoon dried goji berries
- Salt, to taste
- 12 cups cold water

Preparation:
1. In a bowl of water, soak the seaweed for at least 3 hours.
2. In another large bowl of cold water, soak the pork ribs for about 1 hour.
3. Drain the pork ribs and rinse under cold running water completely.
4. In a large pan of boiling water, cook the pork ribs for about 1 minute.
5. Remove from the heat and drain the pork ribs. Set aside.
6. Drain the seaweed and rinse under cold running water completely.
7. In a large soup pan, add all ingredients over high heat and bring it to boil.
8. Reduce the heat to low and simmer, covered for about 4-5 hours.
9. Serve hot.

Serving Suggestions: You can serve this soup with the garnishing of scallion.
Variation Tip: make sure to peel and cut the lotus root just before cooking of soup.
Nutritional Information per Serving:
Calories: 238 | Fat: 13.6g|Sat Fat: 4.8g|Carbohydrates: 8g|Fiber: 1.4g|Sugar: 0.4g|Protein: 21.5g

Tasty Tomato Egg Drop Soup

Prep Time: 15 minutes
Cook Time: 15 minutes
Servings: 4
Ingredients:
- 2 tablespoons canola oil

- 10 ounces tomatoes, cut into small chunks
- 2 cups plus 2 tablespoons water, divided
- 1 cup chicken broth
- 2 teaspoons light soy sauce
- ½ teaspoon sesame oil
- Salt, to taste
- ¼ teaspoon ground white pepper
- 1½ teaspoons corn-starch
- 1 egg, beaten lightly
- 1 scallion, chopped finely
- 2 tablespoons fresh cilantro, chopped

Preparation:
1. In a soup pan, heat the oil over medium-low heat and stir fry the tomato chunks for about 5 minutes.
2. Add 2 cups of water, broth, soy sauce, sesame oil, salt and white pepper and bring to a boil.
3. Reduce the heat to low and simmer for about 1-2 minutes.
4. Meanwhile, in a small bowl, dissolve the corn-starch in remaining water. Set aside.
5. In the soup pan, add the corn-starch mixture, stirring continuously.
6. Add the beaten egg, stirring gently and continuously.
7. Serve immediately with the garnishing of scallions and cilantro.

Serving Suggestions: Serve with the drizzling of lemon juice.
Variation Tip: You can use broth in this recipe.
Nutritional Information per Serving:
Calories: 112 | Fat: 9.2g|Sat Fat: 1.1g|Carbohydrates: 4.6g|Fiber: 1g|Sugar: 2.3g|Protein: 3.5g

Tofu & Veggie Soup

Prep Time: 15 minutes
Cook Time: 12 minutes
Servings: 4
Ingredients:
- 8 ounces frozen shepherd's purse
- 4 cups chicken broth
- 1 teaspoon sesame oil
- Salt, to taste
- ¼ teaspoon ground white pepper
- ¼ cup corn-starch
- ¼ cup water
- 7 ounces silken tofu, pressed, drained and cut into ½-inch cubes
- 3 egg whites

Preparation
1. Through a colander, rinse the shepherd's purse completely.
2. With your hands, gently squeeze the water from the shepherd's purse.
3. Then chop the leaves into small pieces. Set aside.
4. In a medium pan, add the chicken broth, sesame oil, salt and white pepper and bring to a gentle simmer.

5. Meanwhile, dissolve the corn-starch in water.
6. In the soup pan, add the corn-starch mixture, stirring continuously.
7. Simmer for about 1 minute, stirring continuously.
8. Add the shepherd's purse and gently stir to combine.
9. Add the tofu cubes and gently stir to combine.
10. Simmer for about 2-4 minutes.
11. Add the beaten egg whites, stirring gently and continuously.
12. Serve hot.
Serving Suggestions: Serve with a drizzling of lime juice.
Variation Tip: You can substitute the shepherd's purse with frozen spinach.
Nutritional Information per Serving:
Calories: 141| Fat: 4.1g|Sat Fat: 0.8g|Carbohydrates: 13.7g|Fiber: 2g|Sugar: 2g|Protein: 11.9g

Chicken & Corn Egg Soup

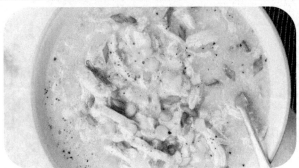

Prep Time: 10 minutes
Cook Time: 12 minutes
Servings: 2
Ingredients:
• 1 teaspoon corn flour
• 1 teaspoon cold water
• 1 (16-ounce) can creamed corn
• 1 garlic clove, minced
• 1 teaspoon fresh ginger, minced
• 1 tablespoon Chinese cooking wine
• 1 teaspoon soy sauce
• 2 cups chicken broth
• 1 cup cooked chicken, shredded
• Salt and ground white pepper, to taste
• 1 egg, beaten
• 3 tablespoons scallions, sliced
Preparation:
1. In a small bowl, dissolve the corn flour in water.
2. In a soup pan, add the creamed corn, garlic, ginger, wine, soy sauce, broth and corn flour mixture over high heat and bring to a boil.
3. Reduce the heat to medium and cook for about 5 minutes, stirring occasionally.
4. Add the cooked chicken, salt and white pepper and cook for about 1-2 minutes.
5. Add the beaten eggs, stirring gently and continuously.
6. Immediately, remove from the heat and serve hot with the garnishing of scallion.
Serving Suggestions: Enjoy with crusty bread.
Variation Tip: For more taste, you can add a little sesame oil in this soup.
Nutritional Information per Serving:
Calories: 355 | Fat: 6.8g|Sat Fat: 1.8g|Carbohydrates: 45.2g|Fiber: 3.2g|Sugar: 8.5g|Protein: 32.5g

Beef & Noodles Soup with Bok Choy

Prep Time: 20 minutes
Cook Time: 2 hours 15 minutes
Servings: 6
Ingredients:
• 2 tablespoons vegetable oil
• ½ pound stewing beef, cubed
• 4 scallions, sliced
• 1 (1-inch) piece fresh ginger, sliced
• 2 garlic cloves, crushed
• 1 splash dry sherry
• Salt and freshly ground black pepper, to taste
• 4 cups beef broth
• 1 cinnamon stick
• 1 star anise
• ½ teaspoon Chinese five-spice powder
• 8 ounces Chinese noodles
• 2 tablespoons low-sodium dark soy sauce
• 1 tablespoon light soy sauce
• 1 tablespoon oyster sauce
• 1 tablespoon fish sauce
• 6 Bok choy leaves
• 6 Chinese cabbage leaves, shredded
Preparation:
1. In a large pan, heat the oil over high heat and cook the beef, scallions, ginger and garlic for about 4-5 minutes or until browned completely, stirring frequently.
2. Stir in the sherry, salt and black pepper and cook for about 1 minute, stirring continuously.
3. Stir in the broth, cinnamon stick, star anise and five-spice powder and bring to a boil.
4. Reduce the heat to low and simmer, covered for about 1-2 hours.
5. Meanwhile, in a pan of boiling water, cook the noodles according to the package instructions.
6. Uncover the pan and discard the ginger, garlic slices and whole spices.
7. Stir in all sauces and again bring to a boil over medium-high heat.
8. Add the Bok choy and cabbage into the soup and cook for about 2-3 minutes.
9. Drain the noodles completely and divide into serving bowls.
10. Top with soup mixture and serve hot.
Serving Suggestions: Serve with the topping of some chili oi.
Variation Tip: You can use chicken broth instead of beef broth.
Nutritional Information per Serving:
Calories: 357 | Fat: 19.6g|Sat Fat: 3.8g|Carbohydrates: 26.5g|Fiber: 2.7g|Sugar: 2g|Protein: 19.6g

Pork Meatballs & Winter Melon Soup

Prep Time: 14 minutes
Cook Time: 15 minutes
Servings: 8
Ingredients:
For meatballs:
- 1 pound ground pork
- 1 scallion, chopped finely
- 1 tablespoon fresh ginger, minced
- 1 egg white
- 2½ tablespoons light soy sauce
- 2 tablespoons Shaoxing wine
- 2 tablespoons water
- 1 teaspoon sesame oil
- ½ teaspoon sugar
- ½ teaspoon ground white pepper
- Salt, to taste
For soup:
- 1½ ounces glass noodles
- 1 tablespoon vegetable oil
- 2 scallions (white parts), chopped
- 1 pound winter melon, peeled and cut into ¼-inch thick chunks
- 4 cups chicken broth
- 2 cups water
- ½ teaspoon sesame oil
- ½ teaspoon ground white pepper
- Salt, to taste
- ¼ cup fresh cilantro, chopped
Preparation:
1. For meatballs: in the bowl of an electric mixer, fitted with the paddle attachment, add all ingredients and mix on low speed for about 6-7 minutes.
2. With lightly greased hands, make equal-sized meatballs from the mixture.
3. Arrange the meatballs onto a lightly greased baking sheet in a single layer and refrigerate for 10-20 minutes.
4. In a bowl of cold water, soak the glass noodles for about 15 minutes.
5. Drain the noodles and cut in half lengthwise. Set aside.
6. In a large soup pan, heat oil over medium heat and sauté the white parts of scallions for about 1 minute.
7. Add winter melon, broth and water and bring to a boil.
8. Place the meatballs with sesame oil and white pepper and again bring to a boil.
9. Add the glass noodles and stir to combine.
10. Cook for about 3-4 minutes.
11. Serve hot with the garnishing of cilantro.
Serving Suggestions: Serve with the topping of soy sauce.

Variation Tip: You can also use ground beef in this soup.
Nutritional Information per Serving:
Calories: 174 | Fat: 5.4g|Sat Fat: 1.4g|Carbohydrates: 11.1g|Fiber: 0.8g|Sugar: 5.3g|Protein: 18.6g

Pork & Shrimp Wonton Soup

Prep Time: 20 minutes
Cook Time: 10 minutes
Servings: 8
Ingredients:
- ½ pound boneless pork loin, chopped roughly
- 2 ounces shrimp, peeled, deveined and chopped finely
- 2 tablespoons plus 1 teaspoon scallions, chopped finely and divided
- 1 teaspoon fresh ginger root, chopped
- 1 tablespoon light soy sauce
- 1 tablespoon Chinese rice wine
- 1 teaspoon brown sugar
- 24 (3½-inch square) wonton wrappers
- 6 cups chicken broth
Preparation:
1. In a large bowl, add the pork, shrimp, 1 teaspoon of the scallion, ginger, soy sauce, wine and sugar and mix until well combined.
2. Set aside for about 25-30 minutes.
3. Arrange 1 wonton wrapper onto a smooth surface.
4. Place about 1 teaspoon of the filling onto the center of 1 wonton wrapper.
5. With wet fingers, moisten the edges of the wrapper.
6. Carefully, pull the top corner down to the bottom and fold the wrapper over the filling to make a triangle.
7. With your fingers, press edges firmly to seal the filling.
8. Now, bring left and right corners together above the filling and then overlap the tips of these corners.
9. With wet fingers, moisten press together.
10. Repeat with the remaining wrappers and filling.
11. In a pan, add the broth and bring to a rolling boil.
12. Carefully, place the wontons in broth and cook for about 5 minutes.
13. Serve hot with the garnishing of the remaining scallion.
Serving Suggestions: Serve with the topping of sambal oelek.
Variation Tip: Feel free to use meat of your choice.
Nutritional Information per Serving:
Calories: 361 | Fat: 3.6g|Sat Fat: 0.9g|Carbohydrates: 56.9g|Fiber: 1.8g|Sugar: 0.9g|Protein: 22.1g

Desserts Recipes

Chinese Mini Egg Cake

Prep Time: 10 minutes.
Cook Time: 20 minutes.
Serves: 12
Ingredients:
- 2 middle size eggs, at room temperature
- ½ cup cake flour,
- 3 tablespoons plus 1 teaspoon castor sugar, around
- ¾ teaspoon olive oil
- warm water

Preparation:
1. Preheat the oven to 180 ° C by 350 degrees F.
2. Prepare a larger bowl and add half of the lukewarm water, then place your bowl on the lukewarm water. Add the eggs and powdered sugar. Beat on medium speed until light and fluffy. Then use the slow speed to remove a few large bubbles. This step is the key to success and it can take 12 to 15 minutes for the mix to reach the group stage.
3. Shift the flour. Then mix well with a spatula. And finally add the oil and mix well.
4. Prepare a mini-12 foil lined muffin pan and pour the batter into it.
5. Cook on the middle rack for 15 to 20 minutes, until the top is nicely coloured.
Serving Suggestion: Serve the egg cake with chips.
Variation Tip: Use powdered sugar.
Nutritional Information Per Serving:
Calories 45 | Fat 1g |Sodium 10mg | Carbs 7g | Fiber 0g | Sugar 3g | Protein 1g

Mango Pudding with Coconut

Prep Time: 15 minutes.
Cook Time: 05 minutes.
Serves:4
Ingredients:
- 1 medium to large ripe mangoes
- ¼ cup water
- 1¼ teaspoons plain gelatin
- ⅙ cup granulated sugar
- ½ cup good-quality coconut milk
- Shaved coconut, optional

Preparation:
1. Cut the mango into pieces and remove the flesh from the skin, including around the stone. Put the mango pulp in a food processor or blender and blend it into a smooth puree. Leave the handle in the machine.
2. Bring the water to a boil in a saucepan. Put out the fire. Stir the water with a whisk or fork, sprinkle the gelatin on the surface and stir vigorously to prevent lumps from forming.
3. Add the sugar to the hot water / gelatin mixture and stir to dissolve.
4. Add this mixture to the mango in the food processor / blender. Add the coconut milk and beat briefly until the ingredients have combined.
5. Pour the pudding into dessert bowls or cups and refrigerate for at least 2 hours (or up to 24 hours if you are cooking ahead).
6. Serve chilled on its own or with a little grated coconut on top.
Serving Suggestion: Serve the Mango Pudding with noodles.
Variation Tip: Use regular milk if not getting coconut milk.
Nutritional Information Per Serving:
Calories 190 | Fat 5.3g |Sodium 48mg | Carbs 33g | Fiber 2.8g | Sugar 30.5g | Protein 4g

Fortune Cake

Prep Time: 10 minutes.
Cook Time: 30 minutes.
Serves: 4
Ingredients:
- 2 cups all-purpose flour
- 1½ cup hot water
- 1 cup brown sugar
- 4 teaspoons baking powder

Preparation:
1. Melt the brown sugar with hot water and set aside.
2. Mix the flour with the baking powder. Add the sugar water. Mix the dough one way for about 3 to 5 minutes. The longest; the best.
3. Pour the batter into the molds. I recommend using a spoon and pouring the batter directly into the center of the molds from higher places and flattening the batter on its own. Put aside.
4. Bring enough water to a boil in a large wok or deep saucepan, prepare the steamer and add the batter when the water begins to boil. I would suggest adding more water to the level just below the shapes.
5. Cover the lid and steam for about 20 to 25 minutes. Flowering should take about 10 minutes. So

use high heat for the first 10 minutes and you can choose to slow the heat down a bit or use high heat throughout the process.

Serving Suggestion: Serve the Fortune Cake with sandwich.

Variation Tip: Use almond flour if gluten free option.

Nutritional Information Per Serving:
Calories 440 | Fat 1g |Sodium 23mg | Carbs 103g | Fiber 1g | Sugar 53g | Protein 7g

Fantastic Egg Tarts

Prep Time: 20 minutes
Cook Time: 30 minutes
Servings: 12
Ingredients:
- ⅔ cup hot water
- ⅓ cup plus 1 tablespoon white sugar
- 1 sheet puff pastry, thawed and refrigerated
- 2 large eggs
- 1 egg yolk
- ⅓ cup evaporated milk
- ½ teaspoon vanilla extract

Preparation:
1. Preheat the oven to 400 degrees F. arrange a rack in the lower third position of oven.
2. In a bowl, add hot water and sugar and stir until dissolved completely. Set aside to cool.
3. Roll out the pastry dough into 14x14-inch and then with a 4-inch cookie cutter, cut into 12 circles.
4. Arrange the pastry circles into 12 (3x1-inch) foil tart tins.
5. Arrange the foil tins onto a large baking sheet. Set aside.
6. In the bowl of sugar syrup, add the eggs, egg yolk, evaporated milk and vanilla extract and beat until well combined.
7. Through a fine sieve, strain the egg mixture into a large bowl.
8. Carefully pour the egg mixture into tart shells, filling to just below the rim.
9. Bake for about 10-15 minutes or until the edges are lightly brown.
10. Now set the temperature of oven to 350 degrees F and bake for about 10-15 minutes further.
11. Remove from oven and place the tarts onto wire rack for about 10-15 minutes before serving.

Serving Suggestions: Serve with the topping of whipped cream.

Variation Tip: As soon as the custard starts to puff, you need to open the oven door 2-3-inch to prevent the filling from puffing up too much.

Nutritional Information per Serving:
Calories: 165 | Fat: 9.5g |Sat Fat: 2.7g|Carbohydrates: 17g|Fiber: 0.3g|Sugar: 7.9g|Protein: 3.3g

Awesome Chinese Almond Cookies

Prep Time: 15 minutes.
Cook Time: 25 minutes.
Serves: 15
Ingredients:
- 1 cup almond flour
- ¼ teaspoon baking powder
- ¼ teaspoon baking soda
- A pinch salt
- ¼ cup butter
- ¼ cup shortening
- 6 tablespoons white sugar
- 1 egg
- 1 ¼ teaspoons almond extract
- 15 whole almonds (blanched)
- 1 egg (lightly beaten)

Preparation:
1. In a large bowl, combine the flour, baking powder, baking soda and salt together.
2. In a medium bowl, combine butter, shortening, and sugar with an electric mixer.
3. Add the egg and almond extract and beat until well combined.
4. Add to the flour mixture and mix well. Note: the dough will crumble at this point.
5. Use your fingers to shape a dough with the mixture, then shape the dough into 2 rolls or blocks 10 to 12 inches in length.
6. Wrap and refrigerate for 2 hours (this will make it easier to form circles with the dough).
7. Take a log and lightly mark the dough at ¾ inch intervals so that you have 15 pieces and cut the dough.
8. Roll each piece into a ball and place them on a lightly greased baking sheet about 1 ½ inches apart.
9. Place an almond in the center of each cookie and press lightly. Repeat with the rest of the dough.
10. Spread egg cookies and bake for 15 to 18 minutes, until golden brown.
11. Cool and enjoy or store in a sealed container.

Serving Suggestion: Serve the Almond Cookies with tea.

Variation Tip: Use all-purpose flour.

Nutritional Information Per Serving:
Calories 117 | Fat 7.4g |Sodium 58mg | Carbs 11.7g | Fiber 0.4g | Sugar 5.1g | Protein 1.7g

Crispy Fried Bananas

Prep Time: 10 minutes.
Cook Time: 10 minutes.
Serves: 8
Ingredients:
• 8 bananas
• Oil, for deep frying
Frying batter
• 2 eggs white
• 1 cup all-purpose flour, sifted
• ½ cup corn-starch
• ½ teaspoon baking powder
• 1 cup water, ice cold
• ½ tablespoon oil
Preparation:
1. Cut the bananas 1-cm-long, set aside. Bananas for fried plantains.
2. Combine all the ingredients for the fried dough in a large bowl. Stir to combine well. Make sure the dough is smooth. Gently add the bananas to the dough.
3. Heat a small 2-3-inch pan of oil over high heat. The oil is ready when it is fully heated and a swirl of smoke rises from the surface.
4. Gently drop each piece of banana into the hot oil. Fry the bananas in portions. Flip the bananas so that both sides are golden and crisp.
5. Remove the fried plantains from the oil using a skimmer and drain them on a plate lined with paper towels.
6. Repeat step 4 until the bananas are gone. Sprinkle a little powdered sugar over the bananas to serve. It can also be served with maple syrup and chocolate sauce.
Serving Suggestion: Serve the Fried bananas with maple syrup and chocolate sauce.
Variation Tip: Use almond flour if want gluten free.
Nutritional Information Per Serving:
Calories 227 | Fat 4g |Sodium 12mg | Carbs 46.5g | Fiber 3.6g | Sugar 14.5g | Protein 3.8g

Traditional Mung Bean Cake

Prep Time: 1 day.
Cook Time: 60 minutes.
Serves:8
Ingredients:
• 1 cup yellow mung beans, unshelled

• ½ cup butter
• ¼ cup vegetable oil
• ½ cup sugar or more if needed, you can slightly adjust this amount
• a small pinch of salt
Coloring
• 5-8 g matcha powder
Preparation:
1. Soak the yellow mung beans overnight. Rinse and dry the next day.
2. In a pressure cooker, add clean water to lightly coat the mung beans and cook using the bean method until the beans are tender and easy to mash. Then crush with a spatula until a smooth and fine mixture is obtained. Place in a non-stick skillet.
3. Add a pinch of salt, butter and vegetable oil to the mung bean mixture. Heat over medium-fine heat and continue to stir. Add the sugar when the oil is well absorbed. Keep stirring until they can easily stick. Put out the fire.
Optional coloring
4. Divide the dough into two equal portions, then transfer one portion. Add about 5-8 g of matcha powder to the other serving and mix well.
Shape and form
5. Then pour the mixture into a colander and press with a spatula. You will see how you come out through the little holes. This step can provide a super smooth and fine texture.
6. Divide the mixture into small doughs of about 30g to 40g, then wrap 10 toppings if you prefer to have a little. Shape it with a moon cake pan or whatever shape you prefer. You should do this step when the mixture is not hot but is still hot.
Serving Suggestion: Serve the Mung Bean Cake with noodles.
Variation Tip: For vegan skip butter.
Nutritional Information Per Serving:
Calories 405 | Fat 16.4g |Sodium 430mg | Carbs 51g | Fiber 12.5g | Sugar 22g | Protein 14.1g

Aromatic Chinese Sesame Cookie

Prep Time: 20 minutes.
Cook Time: 20 minutes.
Serves: 10
Ingredients:
• 1 cup all-purpose flour
• ⅛ teaspoon baking powder
• ¼ teaspoon baking soda
• ⅛ teaspoon salt
• ¼ cup butter (softened)
• ¼ cup shortening
• ⅛ cup white sugar
• ⅛ cup brown sugar
• 1 egg
• ½ teaspoon almond extract
• ¼ cup white sesame seeds (as needed)
Preparation:

1. Sift flour, baking powder, baking soda and salt into a medium bowl.
2. In a large bowl, use an electric mixer to beat the butter, shortening, and white and brown sugars.
3. Add the egg and almond extract and beat until combined.
4. Add the flour mixture and mix well. The dough will be dry and crumbly at this point.
5. Use your fingers to shape a dough with the mixture, then shape the dough into 2 rolls or blocks 10 to 12 inches in length. Package and refrigerate for at least 2 hours, preferably 4 hours. (If you want, you can make the dough ahead of time and refrigerate overnight.)
6. Preheat the oven to 325 degrees F.
7. Take a log and lightly mark the dough at ¾-inch intervals so that you have 15 pieces and cut the dough.
8. Roll each piece into a small ball and roll the ball in the sesame bowl to coat it. (Note: If you wish, you can brush the ball with lightly beaten egg before dipping the sesame seeds in so that the seeds stick to the cookie.)
9. Place the balls on a lightly greased baking sheet, about 5 cm apart.
10. Bake cookies at 325 degrees for about 15 to 17 minutes, or until a fork inserted in the center comes out clean and they can be easily removed from the baking sheet. Let cool completely.
11. Once completely cooled, enjoy or store in an airtight container.

Serving Suggestion: Serve the Chinese Sesame Cookie with tea.
Variation Tip: Use almond flour if want gluten free.
Nutritional Information Per Serving:
Calories 300| Fat 18.1g |Sodium 164mg | Carbs 32g | Fiber 0.6g | Sugar 15.6g | Protein 1.7g

Mouth-watering Raspberry Snowflake Cake

Prep Time: 05 minutes.
Cook Time: 20 minutes.
Serves: 8
Ingredients:
Raspberry snowflake cake
• 2 ounces raspberries
• 15 ⅓ ounces water
• 7 ounces (200 grams) superfine sugar
• 5 leaves gelatin
• 7 ⅛ ounces whole milk
• 2 ounces double cream
• 4 ½ ounces potato starch or corn flour
• 3 ½ ounces water
• 3 tablespoons desiccated coconut

Preparation:
1. Bring the raspberries, 450 ml of water and the extra fine sugar to a boil in a small saucepan. Keep stirring during cooking so that the sugar and raspberries dissolve.
2. Soak the gelatin in cold water.
3. Add the milk and cream to the cooked raspberry jam and bring to a boil again. After cooking, simply turn off the heat and let sit for 10 minutes.
4. Add the gelatin and continue beating so that it mixes evenly.
5. Mix the potato starch and the additional 100 millilitres of water evenly and add them to the raspberry gelatin mixture.
6. Place a sheet of parchment paper on a baking sheet. Pour the mixture into this tray and let stand a few hours in the refrigerator to form.
7. Cut the snowflake cake and cover with grated coconut and it's ready to serve.

Serving Suggestion: Serve the Raspberry Snowflake Cake with chips.
Variation Tip: Use almond milk.
Nutritional Information Per Serving:
Calories 347 | Fat 17.1g |Sodium 33mg | Carbs 45.6g | Fiber 3g | Sugar 28.5g | Protein 6.7g

Chinese Sesame Seed Balls

Prep Time: 15 minutes.
Cook Time: 15 minutes.
Serves: 5
Ingredients:
• 3 cups oil for deep-frying, or as needed
• ¼ cup white sesame seeds, or as needed
• 6 tablespoons packed brown sugar
• ½ cup boiling water
• 1½ cups glutinous rice flour
• ½ cup red bean paste (may not all be used)
Preparation:
1. In a wok or thick, deep pan, begin heating the oil to 250 degrees F. Make sure there is at least 3 inches of oil in the wok.
2. Spread the sesame seeds on a sheet of wax or baking paper. Place a small bowl of water next to the sesame seeds.
3. Dissolve the brown sugar in 1 cup of boiling water.
4. Put the rice flour in a large bowl. Make a hole in the middle and add the mixture of water and dissolved sugar. Stir until you have a sticky caramel-colored paste and add as much of the remaining ⅓ cup of boiling water as needed (don't add water if you don't need it).
5. Pinch off a piece of dough the size of a golf ball. Use your thumb to make a deep indentation in the

dough, then use the thumb and forefinger of both hands to shape the dough into a cup.

6. Roll 1 level teaspoon of sweet red bean paste into a ball. Put the red bean paste in the hole and shape the paste on it to seal it. Make sure the red bean paste is completely covered. Proceed with the rest of the dough.

7. Dip one scoop at a time into the small bowl of water (this will keep the sesame seeds sticking to the dough).

8. Roll the ball over the sesame seeds. Repeat with the remaining balls of dough.

9. Gradually add the sesame balls to the hot oil.

10. Once the sesame seeds have turned light brown (about 2 minutes), use the back of a spatula or large ladle to gently press the balls against the side of the wok or pan. Continue to apply pressure as the balls turn brown and grow to about 3 times their normal size.

11. Drain the fried sesame balls on paper towels.

12. Serve hot and enjoy.

Serving Suggestion: Serve the Sesame Seed Dessert Balls with chocolate sauce.

Variation Tip: Use normal rice flour if not getting glutinous rice flour.

Nutritional Information Per Serving:
Calories 145 | Fat 10.6g |Sodium 4mg | Carbs 12.4g | Fiber 0g | Sugar 10.5g | Protein 1g

Refreshing Soy Milk Pudding

Prep Time: 05 minutes.
Cook Time: 20 minutes.
Serves: 8
Ingredients:
• ¾ cup soybeans, pre-soaked until softened
• 6 cups water
• 2 cups coconut milk
• ⅓ cup sugar or to taste
• 6 pieces of gelatin sheets
Preparation:
Make soy milk
1. Soak the soybeans for 4 hours or until tender. If you plan to soak them overnight, be sure to put them in the fridge.
2. Put the soaked soybeans in the blender, then add water. Mix well. Drain to obtain the soy milk and remove the pulp.
To make the pudding
3. Soak the gelatin pieces in cold water until they soften.
4. Put the soy milk in a saucepan, bring to a boil (stir from time to time to prevent the bottom from sticking). Then simmer for 15 minutes. Turn off the heat, pour in milk or coconut milk. Then the temperature of soy milk drops rapidly. Add the sugar and gelatin. Mix well until the gelatin is dissolved.
5. Filter and distribute in containers. Refrigerate until stiff (takes about 2-4 hours).
To serve

6. Sift or soy bean flour or top and then serve along with soy bean flour.

Serving Suggestion: Serve the Refreshing Soy Milk Pudding with chips.

Variation Tip: Use regular milk.

Nutritional Information Per Serving:
Calories 171 | Fat 14g |Sodium 48mg | Carbs 12g | Fiber 1g | Sugar 9g | Protein 4g

Sesame Red Bean Balls

Prep Time: 20 minutes
Cook Time: 26 minutes
Servings: 8
Ingredients:
• 1½ cups glutinous rice flour, divided
• ⅓ cup granulated sugar
• ¼ cup boiling water
• ¼ cup plus 1 tablespoon cold water (room temperature)
• 7 ounces red bean paste
• ¼ cup sesame seeds, toasted
• 2 cups vegetable oil
Preparation:
1. For dough: in a bowl, add ½ cup of glutinous rice flour and sugar and mix well.
2. Add the boiling water and with a rubber spatula, mix until smooth.
3. Set aside for about 5 minutes.
4. Add the remaining glutinous flour and cold water and mix until a dough forms.
5. Place the dough in a silicone bag and set aside for about 30 minutes.
6. Roll the red bean paste into 8 small balls and set aside.
7. Make 8 balls from the dough.
8. With your hands, flatten each dough ball into a 3-inch disc.
9. Arrange 1 red bean paste ball in the center of each dough ball.
10. Then wrap the dough around the paste ball to cover completely.
11. With your hands, shape the dough into a ball.
12. Through a strainer, rinse the sesame seeds completely and drain well.
13. With kitchen towels, pat dry the sesame seeds slightly.
14. In a shallow plate, place the moistened sesame seeds.
15. Coat each ball with sesame seeds evenly.
16. Then roll the ball in your hands to press the sesame seeds into the dough.
17. In a deep pan, heat the oil to 320 degrees F.
18. Add 4 sesame balls into the oil and cook for about 10 minutes, frequently stirring in a circular motion with a slotted spoon.

19. After 10 minutes of cooking, cook for about 3 minutes, stirring and gently pressing the balls occasionally.
20. Increase the heat slightly and fry for about 5 minutes more, stirring occasionally.
21. With a slotted spoon, transfer the balls onto a paper towel-lined wire rack to drain.
22. Repeat with the remaining balls.
23. Serve warm.
Serving Suggestions: Serve with sweet dipping sauce.
Variation Tip: Peanut oil can also be used for frying.
Nutritional Information per Serving:
Calories: 674 | Fat: 572g|Sat Fat: 11.1g|Carbohydrates: 37.8g|Fiber: 1.2g|Sugar: 8.4g|Protein: 3.8g

Classic Tapioca Pudding with Taro

Prep Time: 15 minutes
Cook Time: 35 minutes
Servings: 6
Ingredients:
• 6 cups water, divided
• 1½ pounds taro, peeled and cut into ½ inch pieces
• ½ cup tapioca pearls
• 1 (13.7-ounce) can coconut milk
• 1 cup sugar
Preparation:
1. In a medium pan, add 4 cups of water and taro over high heat and bring to a boil.
2. Reduce the heat to medium and cook for about 20 minutes.
3. Remove from the heat and drain the water.
4. With a fork, mash the taro pieces slightly.
5. Meanwhile, in a small pan, add remaining water and bring to a boil.
6. Stir in the tapioca pearls and cook for about 6 minutes.
7. Remove from the heat and set the pan aside, covered for about 10-15 minutes, or until the pearls are translucent.
8. Through a colander, strain the tapioca pearls and rinse under cold running water.
9. Return the tapioca pearls into the pan with coconut milk, taro, and sugar and mix well.
10. Place the pan over medium heat and cook for about 2-3 minutes or until sugar dissolves completely, stirring continuously.
11. Remove from the heat and set aside to cool slightly.
12. Serve either warm.
Serving Suggestions: Serve with the topping of fresh fruit.
Variation Tip: Don't mash the taro pieces like mashed potatoes.
Nutritional Information per Serving:
Calories: 465 | Fat: 15.6g|Sat Fat: 13.8g|Carbohydrates: 83.7g|Fiber: 7.2g|Sugar:

Awesome Banana Fritters

Prep Time: 15 minutes
Cook Time: 16 minutes
Servings: 8
Ingredients:
• ½ cup water
• ½ cup all-purpose flour
• ½ cup corn-starch
• 2 tablespoons milk
• 1 tablespoon butter, melted
• 1 tablespoon granulated sugar
• 4 large ripe bananas, peeled and cut into 1-inch chunks
• 1½ cups vegetable oil
• 1 tablespoon powdered sugar
Preparation:
1. In a bowl, add the water, flour, corn-starch, milk, butter, granulated sugar and mix until well combined.
2. Add the banana chunks and coat with the mixture evenly.
3. In a deep skillet, heat oil over medium-high heat and fry the banana chunks in 4 batches for about 2-4 minutes or until golden brown.
4. With a slotted spoon, transfer the banana chunks onto a wire rack lined plate to drain.
5. Set aside to cool down slightly.
6. Serve with the sprinkling of powdered sugar.
Serving Suggestions: Serve with whipping cream.
Variation Tip: Make sure to use ripe bananas.
Nutritional Information per Serving:
Calories: 497 | Fat: 42.7g|Sat Fat: 9.1g|Carbohydrates: 29.4g|Fiber: 1.8g|Sugar: 9.9g|Protein: 1.6g

Aromatic Mango Pudding

Prep Time: 15 minutes
Servings: 4
Ingredients:
• ½ cup hot water
• 3 teaspoons gelatin
• ⅓ cup white sugar
• 2 large ripe mangoes, peeled, pitted and sliced
• 1 cup coconut milk

Preparation:
1. In a bowl, add the boiling water and gelatin and beat vigorously until dissolved.
2. Add the sugar and stir until dissolved.
3. In a food processor, add the mango and pulse until smooth.
4. Add the gelatin mixture and coconut milk and pulse until well combined.
5. Transfer the pudding into serving bowls and refrigerate for about 4-6 hours before serving.
Serving Suggestions: Serve with the garnishing of fresh fruit of your choice.
Variation Tip: Use sweet mangoes.
Nutritional Information per Serving:
Calories: 310 | Fat: 14.9g|Sat Fat: 12.8g|Carbohydrates: 45.2g|Fiber: 4g|Sugar: 41.6g|Protein: 5g

Chinese Soy Bean Pudding

Prep Time: 10 minutes
Cook Time: 15 minutes
Servings: 6
Ingredients:
For pudding:
• 4 cups soy milk
• 1 tablespoon agar-agar powder
• ½ cup water
• 2 teaspoons vanilla extract
For syrup:
• ¾ cup water
• ½ cup sugar
• 1 (1-inch) piece fresh ginger, smashed
Preparation:
1. For pudding: in a medium pan, add soy milk over medium heat and cook for about 2-3 minutes or until warmed.
2. In another pan, add ½ cup of water over medium heat and ring to a boil.
3. Add agar-agar powder and stir until dissolved.
4. Stir in the warm soy milk and vanilla extract and bring to a gentle boil, stirring continuously.
5. Remove from the heat and through a strainer, strain the mixture into a large pan.
6. With a clean kitchen towel, warp the lid tightly.
7. Then cover the pan with lid and set aside to cool slightly.
8. Refrigerate the pan for about 2 hours.
9. For syrup: in a small pan, add all ingredients over medium heat and cook for about 3-5 minutes or until sugar is dissolved, stirring continuously.
10. Remove from the heat and discard the ginger.

11. Remove the pan of pudding from the refrigerator and with a flat spatula, cut into thin slices.
12. Top with sugar syrup and serve.
Serving Suggestions: Serve with the garnishing of fresh berries.
Variation Tip: Strictly follow the measurement of ingredients for best results.
Nutritional Information per Serving:
Calories: 162 | Fat: 2.9g|Sat Fat: 0.4g|Carbohydrates: 28.8g|Fiber: 1.3g|Sugar: 23.4g|Protein: 5.5g

Yummy Mango Ice Cream

Prep Time: 15 minutes
Cook Time: 5 minutes
Servings: 6
Ingredients:
• 2 cups mango, peeled, pitted and cubed
• ½ plus ⅓ cup granulated sugar, divided
• 2-2½ tablespoons fresh lime juice
• 1¾ cups half-and-half
• 1¼ cups coconut milk
Preparation:
1. In a large bowl, add the mango cubes and ⅓ cup of sugar and mix well.
2. Cover the bowl and refrigerate overnight.
3. In a pan, add mango mixture over medium-low heat and cook for about 5 minutes, stirring occasionally.
4. Remove from the heat and set aside to cool.
5. In a blender, add the mango mixture and pulse until smooth.
6. Add the lime juice and pulse until combined.
7. Transfer the mango puree into a bowl and refrigerate, covered for about 1 hour.
8. In a large bowl, add half-and-half, coconut milk and remaining sugar and beat until well combined and sugar dissolves completely.
9. Add the mango puree and gently stir to combine.
10. Transfer the mango mixture into a freezer-safe container and freeze for at least 6 hours, stirring occasionally.
Serving Suggestions: Serve with the garnishing of toasted coconut and fresh mint leaves.
Variation Tip: You can adjust the amount of sugar according to the tartness of mangoes.
Nutritional Information per Serving:
Calories: 334 | Fat: 20.3g|Sat Fat: 15.7g|Carbohydrates: 39.1g|Fiber: 2g|Sugar: 34.3g|Protein: 3.7g

Conclusion

It is a common misconception that Chinese food makes you fat and therefore unhealthy. Of course, it's no surprise if your experience was limited to fried spring rolls or sweet and sour chicken in a batter with a thick, sweet sauce. But do the Chinese really live on a daily fried diet?

The answer, of course, is no. There are many different methods of Chinese cooking. Let's explore a few here. The Chinese tend to eat around 2 to 3 dishes per meal, which can help with a variety of essential nutrients. At the same time, eating is more fun because you can experience many different flavors and textures. It could be a tangy hot soup or a crisp and refreshing cold salad alongside the ubiquitous smooth, hearty rice.

Here is an important point. The Chinese regard food as a medicine. Some of the most important ingredients in Chinese cuisine are ginger, garlic, chives, and chili peppers. All of them have been shown to have great health benefits. If you have a cold, the Chinese tell you to eat raw garlic or drink ginger tea. And if you have a sore throat, the Chinese will probably make dessert pear soup for you. Most of the time when Chinese people have stomach problem, they probably eat a lot of porridge and soup. However, Chinese porridge is not made from oats, but from a mixture of grains like rice, green beans or barley. It also tends to be "thicker". Needless to say, it's delicious! Liquid foods fill naturally so that they don't necessarily leave marks on the waistline!

Another essential part of the Chinese diet is three good meals a day, and they tend to fill you up. In other words, the Western obsession to clean everything on the plate is not really on the Chinese table.

Appendix Measurement Conversion Chart

WEIGHT EQUIVALENTS

US STANDARD	METRIC (APPROXIMATE)
1 ounce	28 g
2 ounces	57 g
5 ounces	142 g
10 ounces	284 g
15 ounces	425 g
16 ounces (1 pound)	455 g
1.5 pounds	680 g
2 pounds	907 g

TEMPERATURES EQUIVALENTS

FAHRENHEIT(F)	CELSIUS (C) (APPROXIMATE)
225 °F	107 °C
250 °F	120 °C
275 °F	135 °C
300 °F	150 °C
325 °F	160 °C
350 °F	180 °C
375 °F	190 °C
400 °F	205 °C
425 °F	220 °C
450 °F	235 °C
475 °F	245 °C
500 °F	260 °C

VOLUME EQUIVALENTS (DRY)

US STANDARD	METRIC (APPROXIMATE)
⅛ teaspoon	0.5 mL
¼ teaspoon	1 mL
½ teaspoon	2 mL
¾ teaspoon	4 mL
1 teaspoon	5 mL
1 tablespoon	15 mL
¼ cup	59 mL
½ cup	118 mL
¾ cup	177 mL
1 cup	235 mL
2 cups	475 mL
3 cups	700 mL
4 cups	1 L

VOLUME EQUIVALENTS (LIQUID)

US STANDARD	US STANDARD (OUNCES)	METRIC (APPROXIMATE)
2 tablespoons	1 fl.oz	30 mL
¼ cup	2 fl.oz	60 mL
½ cup	4 fl.oz	120 mL
1 cup	8 fl.oz	240 mL
1½ cup	12 fl.oz	355 mL
2 cups or 1 pint	16 fl.oz	475 mL
4 cups or 1 quart	32 fl.oz	1 L
1 gallon	128 fl.oz	4 L

Printed in Great Britain
by Amazon

21946201R00044